Twayne's English Authors Series

Sylvia E. Bowman, *Editor*

INDIANA UNIVERSITY

Edward FitzGerald

TEAS 205

Edward FitzGerald

EDWARD FITZGERALD

By IRAN B. HASSANI JEWETT

GEORGE PRIOR PUBLISHERS
London, England
TWAYNE PUBLISHERS
A Division of G. K. Hall & Co.
Boston, Massachusetts, U. S. A.

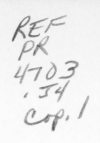

Library of Congress Cataloging in Publication Data

Jewett, Iran B   Hassani.
  Edward FitzGerald.

  (Twayne's English authors series ; TEAS 205)
  Bibliography: pp. 165–70
  Includes index.
  1. FitzGerald, Edward, 1809–1883.   2. Authors,
English—19th century—Biography.
PR4703.J4   821'.8   76-30375
ISBN 0-8057-6675-8

This edition is published in the United Kingdom by George Prior
Publishers, Rugby Chambers, 2 Rugby Street, London, WC1,
England.

          ISBN 0-86043-091-X

Contents

About the Author

Iran B. Hassani Jewett had the good fortune to be born in a family of Iranian scholars. Her parents were both college professors in the state of Hyderabad, India, ruled then by the Nizam. Her father, a linguist, received wide recognition for his dictionary of the Persian language, *Farhange Nizam*.

The author has a Ph. D. in English and American literature from the University of Maryland, and an M. A. in English from Georgetown University. Her undergraduate studies were completed in India, and she spent a number of years studying in Iran.

The author has taught English literature; she has written for the radio and for periodicals in the U. S. A., India and Iran. Her articles on comparative literature have appeared in scholarly journals such as *Orientalia Suecana* and *Oriens*. She is the Persian editor of Twayne's World Authors Series, and is completing a book on the nineteenth century English stylist, Alexander W. Kinglake.

Preface

Since Edward FitzGerald's *Rubáiyát of Omar Khayyám* first saw the light of day in 1859, numerous editions have appeared; and translations of this translation have been made in every language of consequence. The anonymous volume of the quatrains bore the title, *Rubáiyát of Omar Khayyám, the Astronomer-Poet of Persia, Translated into English Verse;* and the translator explained in the preface that his version differed from the original in that he had strung the independent stanzas of the Persian into "something of an Eclogue," with a less than equal proportion of the drink and make merry. He might have added that his work was not a translation in the strict sense of the word but the re-creation in English of the literary qualities of the Persian. As FitzGerald would explain in his letters, he was trying to capture, not the mere form or meaning of the original but its essential beauty; he was striving to produce the effect in English that Omar had achieved in his language. For the sake of quality FitzGerald was willing to sacrifice fidelity. "Better a live Sparrow than a stuffed Eagle," was his motto. The long-lasting popularity of the *Rubáiyát* has proved that it was not a sparrow, as its creator modestly assumed, but a royal eagle.

While keeping in mind the fact that FitzGerald's works are to an extent translations, it is primarily as English poems and plays that they can be truly appreciated. As a translation, the *Rubáiyát* has been scrutinized and analyzed extensively; Edward Heron-Allen's analysis of FitzGerald's *Rubáiyát* published in 1899 examined the English version stanza by stanza and listed the Persian quatrains that resembled the English. Other scholars since then have studied FitzGerald's version closely, hoping to uncover any fresh sources that Heron-Allen may have overlooked. Needless to say, the field has been well researched, and any further elaboration on the matter of FitzGerald's divergence from the Persian would be redundant. This volume, therefore, focusses attention on the aspect of the *Rubáiyát* that has not been sufficiently explored: its merits as an English poem. A detailed study is presented of the original features that FitzGerald introduced into the *Rubáiyát* and the literary devices that he employed to evoke in his readers changes of mood in keeping with the theme of his "Epicurean Eclogue." The analysis should help to create a greater awareness of the beauty of this English masterpiece.

FitzGerald did not write for fame or money; he wrote only to please himself and, sometimes, to please his friends. Friendship played an important part in FitzGerald's literary life, and thus no discussion of his work would be complete without an account of these deep and lasting relationships. FitzGerald's other writings have not been overlooked; though none of them approach the stature of the *Rubáiyát*, they are not without merit. His translations from the Spanish and the Greek classics have been judged on their intrinsic merits of dramatic force and graceful diction. FitzGerald himself made no pretence of fidelity to the original works, and no attempt is made in this book to analyze his plays as translations. FitzGerald's adaptations from two famous Persian poems, *Salámán and Absál* and *Bird Parliament*, should prove interesting to the reader because of their mystical philosophy and the contrast they present to the *Rubáiyát*. Since none of FitzGerald's minor works are well-known, discussions of their merits and shortcomings are liberally illustrated with quotations. In addition, every effort is made to allow the reader to hear in FitzGerald's own words his views of what he wrote and translated and the method he followed.

In regard to the transcription of Persian names, diacritical marks are omitted, except in quotations and in the titles of books and articles. Since there are no standard rules of transcription, traditional spellings that come as close as possible to the Persian are employed. It may be helpful to add that the capitalization of nouns in FitzGerald's writings was his personal idiosyncracy and carries no special significance.

Iran B. Hassani Jewett

Washington, D. C.

Chronology

CHAPTER 1

Childhood and Youth

I *Early Years*

EDWARD FitzGerald was born Edward Purcell on March 31, 1809. The house in which he was born, the White House, later called Bredfield House, was located seven miles north of Ipswich between Woodbridge and Bredfield village. Though FitzGerald ranged far and wide in his reading, and traveled in imagination to the Greece of Aeschylus, to the Spain of Calderon, and to the Persia of Omar Khayyam, he spent most of his life in the vicinity of his birthplace.

FitzGerald's parents were Irish. His father, John Purcell, was the son of a wealthy physician of Dublin and a descendant of the barons of Loughmoe. His Anglo-Norman ancestors had entered England in the army of William the Conqueror and had then crossed over to Ireland where they had settled. John Purcell had studied at Trinity College, Dublin, and enrolled in the Inner Temple in London. Being a gentleman of means, however, he had not found it necessary to practice law. After marriage he settled at Bredfield and devoted himself to politics and to the various duties of a country squire.

Edward's mother, Mary Frances FitzGerald, was John Purcell's first cousin and an heiress in her own right. The FitzGeralds were very proud of their lineage. Their ancestor, Otho Geraldino, a descendant of the dukes of Tuscany, had been a trusted commander under William the Conqueror; and, for his services in the invasion of England, had been rewarded by that monarch with the title of baron. Later the FitzGeralds had sought fame and fortune in Ireland, and had succeeded in finding both. In 1315 when the Scots invaded Ireland, John FitzThomas FitzGerald of Kildare had fought back the invaders, and for his bravery received the earldom of Kil-

11

dare from a grateful Edward II. Maurice, the fourth earl of Kildare, was the founder of Edward FitzGerald's branch of the family.

For five centuries, the earls of Kildare played an important part in Irish politics, serving in high offices and gaining a reputation for courage and ability. But their disregard for convention and disdain for authority made for them powerful enemies at court, where they were frequently summoned to answer charges brought against them. Apparently their unorthodox manner of answering these complaints succeeded well, for the Kildares continued to wield power, becoming one of the three ruling families of Ireland. The FitzGeralds accumulated large estates, which during the lifetime of FitzGerald's grandfather, John FitzGerald, included properties in Suffolk, Lancashire, and Staffordshire. After John FitzGerald's death in 1818, the family fortune passed to his daughter and sole heir, Mary Frances. The Purcells at the same time changed their name to FitzGerald and adopted the FitzGerald coat of arms.

Though the FitzGeralds owned several houses, they preferred to live at Bredfield House, a large mansion set in pleasant surroundings, which they rented from their friend and neighbour Squire Jenney of Hasketon. Squire Jenney was a frequent guest at Bredfield House and a hunting companion of John FitzGerald. Edward remembered how, as a child, he had looked out the nursery window and seen his father and Squire Jenney in their hunting attire passing across the lawn with their pack of hounds. Another close friend of the family whom FitzGerald always remembered with affection was Major Moore of Bealings House, a retired officer of the British Indian army, who knew Persian and whose hobby was collecting words and phrases peculiar to Suffolk. He had published *Oriental Fragments* and edited *Suffolk Words and Phrases,* and it has been conjectured that he might have inspired FitzGerald to study Persian. FitzGerald himself, however, does not credit Major Moore with starting him on his Persian studies. Moore might also have aroused FitzGerald's interest in the Suffolk dialect, which FitzGerald collected in the 1860s, especially the words and phrases of the sea coast, of which he compiled a vocabulary.

Edward's childhood was uneventful and not very different apparently from that of other children in wealthy households of the period. There were eight children in the FitzGerald family: Mary Frances, who died young; John; Andalusia; Mary Eleanor; Jane; Peter; Edward; and Isabella. Mary Eleanor, who later married John

Kerrich of Geldestone Hall, was FitzGerald's favorite sister. The FitzGerald children spent much of their time in the nursery, which at Bredfield was located at the top of the house. Through the open window the children could hear the bells of the church of St. Mary the Virgin pealing in Woodbridge. The sea, FitzGerald's lifelong love, was only a few miles away. During the Napoleonic wars, the topmasts of Lord Nelson's men-of-war that were anchored in Hollesley Bay could be seen from the house. FitzGerald described the house of this childhood with affectionate nostalgia in his poem "Bredfield Hall," which he wrote when he was about thirty:

> Lo, an English mansion founded
>   In the elder James's reign,
> Quaint and stately, and surrounded
>   With a pastoral domain.
>
> With well-timber'd lawn and gardens
>   And with many a pleasant mead,
> Skirted by the lofty coverts
>   Where the hare and pheasant feed.
>
> Flank'd it is with goodly stables,
>   Shelter'd by coeval trees:
> So it lifts its honest gables
>   Toward the distant German seas;
>
> Where it once discern'd the smoke
>   Of old sea-battles far away:
> Saw victorious Nelson's topmasts
>   Anchoring in Hollesley Bay.
>
> But whatever storm might riot
>   Cannon roar, and trumpet ring,
> Still amid these meadows quiet
>   Did the yearly violet spring:
>
> Still Heaven's starry hand suspended
>   That light balance of the dew,
> That each night on earth descended,
>   And each morning rose anew:
>
> And the ancient house stood rearing
>   Undisturb'd her chimneys high,

And her gilded vanes still veering
    Toward each quarter of the sky:

While like wave to wave succeeding
    Through the world of joy and strife,
Household after household speeding
    Handed on the torch of life:

First, sir Knight in ruff and doublet,
    Arm in arm with stately dame;
Then the Cavaliers indignant
    For their monarch brought to shame:

Languid beauties limn'd by Lely;
    Full-wigg'd Justice of Queen Anne:
Tory squires who tippled freely;
    And the modern Gentleman:

Here they lived, and here they greeted,
    Maids and matrons, sons and sires,
Wandering in its walks, or seated
    Round its hospitable fires:

Oft their silken dresses floated
    Gleaming through the pleasure ground:
Oft dash'd by the scarlet-coated
    Hunter, horse, and dappled hound.

Till the Bell that not in vain
    Had summon'd them to weekly prayer,
Call'd them one by one again
    To the church—and left them there!

They with all their loves and passions,
    Compliments, and song, and jest,
Politics, and sports, and fashions,
    Merged in everlasting rest!

So they pass—while thou, old Mansion,
    Markest with unalter'd face
How like the foliage of thy summers
    Race of man succeeds to race.

To most thou stand'st a record sad,
    But all the sunshine of the year

Could not make thine aspect glad
To one whose youth is buried here.

In thine ancient rooms and gardens
Buried—and his own no more
Than the youth of those old owners,
Dead two centuries before.

Unto him the fields around thee
Darken with the days gone by:
O'er the solemn woods that bound thee
Ancient sunsets seem to die.

Sighs the selfsame breeze of morning
Through the cypress as of old;
Ever at the Spring's returning
One same crocus breaks the mould.

Still though 'scaping Time's more savage
Handywork this pile appears,
It has not escaped the ravage
Of the undermining years.

And though each succeeding master,
Grumbling at the cost to pay,
Did with coat of paint and plaster
Hide the wrinkles of decay;

Yet the secret worm ne'er ceases,
Nor the mouse behind the wall:
Heart of oak will come to pieces,
And farewell to Bredfield Hall!

The poem is weak in parts; stanzas such as the one beginning "Languid beauties limn'd by Lely," would not have escaped alteration if FitzGerald had intended the poem for publication. The poem was circulated among friends in FitzGerald's lifetime, and first published in the posthumous *Letters and Literary Remains* edited by William Aldis Wright. In spite of its imperfections, the poem has passages of beauty which foreshadow the *Rubáiyát*. There is the same sadness at the inevitability of decay and death, though FitzGerald wrote this poem when he was a young man. The stanza describing the morning breeze sighing through the cypress and the

crocus breaking the mold in spring could easily belong to the
Rubáiyát. FitzGerald himself retained a strong affection for this
poem about the house of his childhood. Forty years after he had
composed it, he recited to himself the lines of "Bredfield Hall"
while walking in the garden.

The FitzGerald household during Edward's early years seems to
have been a well-disciplined one that lacked closeness and affection.
Mrs. FitzGerald was a celebrated beauty of her day whose social
activities did not leave her much time for motherly devotion.
The fashionable painter Thomas Lawrence, who made twenty-
three portraits and sketches of her, portrays her as a woman of
aristocratic bearing with large expressive eyes, a long and slender
nose, and a strong chin. She was noted for her wit and eccentricity,
and for the Kildare haughtiness of temper, all of which attributes
she seems to have passed on to her sons in greater or lesser degree.
Her expensive tastes in fur and jewelry were so well-known that
they were the envy of at least one young contemporary, Fanny
Kemble, the daughter of Charles Kemble, the actor-manager of
Covent Garden whose wife was a friend of Mrs. FitzGerald's. In her
Records of a Girlhood Fanny Kemble, who later became a famous
actress, recalls how as a young girl she used to attend Sunday dinner
at the FitzGerald home, where the magnificence of the gold dessert
service and table ornaments made a profound impression upon her.
The gold dishes were replaced when Mrs. FitzGerald wearied of
them by a set of ground glass and dead and burnished silver that was
"so exquisite, that the splendid gold service was pronounced
infinitely less tasteful and beautiful."[1]

Mrs. FitzGerald was very fond of the theater and the opera, and
she stayed during the season at her house in London at 39 Portland
Place. She had a permanent box in the third row of the Opera House
at Haymarket; and, as a young man, Edward FitzGerald often es-
corted his mother to the opera and to the theater. He shared
her liking for both, and he may have inherited his artistic temperament from his mother. But he disliked high society and the
lavish show of splendor for which his mother was noted. He seems
to have retreated to the opposite extreme: on one occasion, when he
was at Trinity College, his mother called on him in her coach-and-
four, and sent a lackey to ask him to step down to the college gate.
But he could not come—his only pair of shoes was at the cobbler's.[2]
Perhaps FitzGerald's extreme shyness and reclusive habits were

reactions against his mother's style of living. It might not be too farfetched to hold his mother responsible, to an extent, for his unhappy and short-lived marriage in middle age to a woman he did not love. As FitzGerald's letters show, his mother's refusal to help him financially was one of the reasons that prevented him from getting married in his youth to a girl he greatly admired.

Even as a child, FitzGerald was fully aware of his mother's shortcomings and felt her neglect deeply. Years later, in a letter to his friend Fanny Kemble, he described the infrequent visits of his mother to the nursery:

My mother used to come up sometimes, and we Children were not much comforted. She was a remarkable woman, as you said in a former letter: and as I constantly believe in outward Beauty as an Index of a Beautiful Soul within, I used sometimes to wonder what feature in her fine face betrayed what was not so good in her Character. I think (as usual) the Lips: there was a twist of Mischief about them now and then, like that in—the Tail of a Cat!—Otherwise so smooth and amiable.[3]

When Edward was seven years old, the FitzGeralds went to France, where they lived for two years, first at Saint-Germain-en-Laye, and then in Paris. The cultural atmosphere of the city and the frequent visits to the Louvre and the theater played an important part in nurturing Edward's artistic bent. In 1818, Mrs. FitzGerald's father died and the family returned to England; and in the autumn of the same year, Edward and his two brothers were enrolled in the King Edward VI Grammar School at Bury St. Edmunds, Suffolk. John, the eldest brother, entered the sixth form; Peter and Edward, the first form.

II *Famous Friendships*

The eight years that Edward FitzGerald spent at Bury St. Edmunds were both pleasant and instructive. The school, regarded as one of the finest in England, was noted especially for the excellence of its classical studies. The headmaster, Dr. Benjamin Heath Malkin, was a broadminded, genial, and humorous man whose strict but fair administration was popular among the students. He had a great appreciation for English literature, and he took care that his pupils not only studied the classics, required for entrance into a university, but also mastered the English language. He drilled them in essay writing and translation, sometimes carrying both to extreme lengths. Under his tutelage FitzGerald acquired the eloquent and graceful style which became the distinguishing mark of his prose and poetry.

The years at Bury St. Edmunds were important to Edward FitzGerald from another point of view also; it was at school that he formed some of his most important friendships. FitzGerald once said that his friendships were like loves; to the end of his life, he maintained an affectionate regard for the friends of his childhood. He did not make friends easily, and those that he considered friends he never forgot. These companions of his youth largely constituted the limited circle of his close friendships.

The men whose names appear most frequently in FitzGerald's correspondence—William Bodham Donne, James Spedding, John Mitchell Kemble, and William Airy—were his school mates at Bury St. Edmunds and his college fellows at Cambridge. They all belonged to the upper strata of society and shared similar interests. Donne was the son of a Norfolk gentleman and a descendant of the poet John Donne; on his mother's side, he was related to William Cowper. Donne became the librarian of the London Library, was appointed Examiner of Plays, occasionally wrote articles and reviews for periodicals, and was one of the three friends to whom FitzGerald sent copies of the *Rubáiyát*.

James Spedding, the son of a wealthy Cumberland farmer, showed such great promise as a young man that his friends expected great accomplishments of him; but, after a brief career in the foreign service, he devoted his time and energy to editing the works of Sir Francis Bacon, and to vindicating his character, a pursuit which his friends, especially FitzGerald, regarded as a waste of talent. Spedding was also a Shakespeare scholar, and his articles about the editing and interpreting of Shakespeare's plays were greatly admired by FitzGerald. John Mitchell Kemble, the son of Charles Kemble and the brother of Fanny Kemble, departed from the family tradition of acting to devote his career to the study of Anglo-Saxon. William Airy, the brother of Astronomer Royal Sir George Airy, became the vicar of Keysoe in Bedfordshire and frequently visited FitzGerald at Woodbridge.

When FitzGerald was seventeen, he entered Trinity College, Cambridge. He had shown himself to be a promising and even an ambitious student during his final year at Bury St. Edmunds where he stood fourth in the final examinations. At Cambridge, however, he showed neither ambition nor effort; he chose a "pass" or ordinary degree rather than an "honours" degree which the more competitive students preferred. FitzGerald's apathy towards scholarly distinction may be explained to a large extent by the nature of the curriculum at the time. The university placed its chief emphasis on mathematics, and it relegated literature to a secondary place. As a result, many students who were not interested in mathematics passed up the honors course. Brilliant men such as Charles Darwin and Thomas Babington Macaulay, who were at Cambridge about the same time as FitzGerald, chose the ordinary degree for the same reason.

If FitzGerald's stay at Cambridge was undistinguished from the point of view of scholarship, it was important in another respect. His closest and most celebrated friendships were formed at Cambridge or in the years immediately following his graduation. It has been remarked that even if FitzGerald had not translated the *Rubáiyát*, his friendships alone would have assured him a place in the literary history of the Victorian era. Tennyson was at Cambridge at the time and belonged to the Conversazione Society or the "Apostles," many of whose members became leading figures of the nineteenth century. FitzGerald's friends from Bury St. Edmunds belonged to this famous society and FitzGerald could have joined at any time, had he wished to do so. The Apostles sympathized with revolutionary movements in Europe, and regarded themselves as men entrusted with the mission of enlightening the world. Their messianic zeal held no attraction for FitzGerald, who even as a young man was inclined to be a skeptic. His own participation in extracurricular activities consisted of membership in a group called "Camus," which gave vocal and musical concerts. FitzGerald, who performed well on the piano, usually took part in the recitals.

If the Apostles were too earnest for FitzGerald's tastes, one young contemporary, William Makepeace Thackeray, possessed qualities dear to FitzGerald: simplicity, sincerity, and above all, humor. FitzGerald was in his last year at college and Thackeray was a freshman when they met for the first time in their tutor's rooms. Their casual meeting soon ripened into a close friendship. Neither was interested in mathematics or ambitious of academic honors. They were both well read in literature, well versed in art and in music, and both liked to sketch. Thackeray's droll fancies were expressed in caricatures designed to please FitzGerald's sense of humor. One such cartoon of those early days depicts Thackeray's idea for a new musical instrument for his friend. Labeled "The Hogmagundy," it depicts a young lady pulling the tails of pigs to produce musical notes.

Endless distractions at Cambridge kept the two friends occupied. FitzGerald, who had stayed somewhat aloof at college, enjoyed himself in Thackeray's company as he had never done before. Their whimsical sense of humor delighted in the understated and the unusual, and they found a perpetual source of enjoyment in the foibles of mankind. FitzGerald later recalled how they had dubbed William Wordsworth, the poet, the "Mēēserable Poet," and William's brother Christopher, the Master of Trinity, the "Mēēserable Sinner," because of his habit of intoning the prayers at chapel in a high nasal voice. The two young friends had nicknames for each other as well. Thackeray was "Old Thack" and "Willy," and FitzGerald "Yedward," "Neddikins," "Teddibus," or anything else depending on Thackeray's whim of the moment. They took long walks in the meadows, and sang humorous songs. A favorite song was "Troll, troll the bonny brown Bowl." After Thackeray's death, FitzGerald set Thackeray's poem, "Ho, Pretty Page," to this tune, and printed copies which he distributed among friends.

In 1830, after FitzGerald had graduated from college, he decided to visit Paris in the spring. He was joined there by Thackeray, who, having acquired the sum of twenty pounds, had left for Paris without telling anyone where he was going. Thackeray recalled the episode many years later in the *Roundabout Papers* in his essay on the Hotel Dessein at Calais. After Thackeray left Cambridge without taking a degree, he stayed with his mother in her home Larkbeare in Devon; and from there he carried on a lengthy correspondence with FitzGerald, embellishing his letters with drawings and cartoons. One sketch is of Larkbeare, with its portico and straight windows, and another shows Thackeray, seated on a mare, his arms folded, looking up at the moon. There are also comfortable little sketches of armchairs by sparkling fires, of kettles singing upon the hob, and of the young artist with curly black hair sitting, writing, or drawing. One cartoon of a little figure who is leaping into bed is captioned, "Here I go, gute nacht, lieber Edward!" FitzGerald, who saved all these sketches with enough of the captions left to explain the pic-

tures, sent them after Thackeray's death to his daughter Anne
Ritchie. She included the drawings in the special Biographical Edition of Thackeray's works. The introductions to the volumes in this
edition were written by her and are based on her recollections of her
father. She devoted the introduction to volume seventeen of the
Biographical Edition to Thackeray's friendship with FitzGerald.

FitzGerald's letters to Thackeray at Larkbeare, which are somewhat in the form of a diary, were added to from day to day and
reflect the mood of the writer. One such letter that has survived
covers a period of five days and ranges over a wide variety of sub-
jects, from books read and walks taken, to a discussion of religion.
FitzGerald's doubts about religion that persisted throughout his life
are eloquently expressed to Thackeray: "If you can prove to me that
one miracle took place, I will believe that he is a just God who
damned us all because a woman eat an apple; & you can't expect
greater complaisance [than] that, to be sure."[4] In the same letter,
written from October 5 to 9, 1831, FitzGerald includes two songs
that he had composed especially for his dear Thackeray at half past
one during the night "when the wind was blowing hard at the windows & I somehow began to think of Will Thackeray: so the cockles
of my heart were warmed, and up spouted the following: I have
drunk a glass of port, & so sit down to transcribe them":

1

I cared not for life: for true friend I had none
I had heard 'twas a blessing not under the sun:
Some figures called friends, hollow, proud, or cold-hearted
Came to me like shadows—like shadows departed:
But a day came that turned all my sorrow to glee
When first I saw Willy, and Willy saw me!

2

The thought of my Willy is always a cheerer;
My wine has new flavour—the fire burns clearer:
The sun ever shines—I am pleased with all things—
And this crazy old world seems to go with new springs;—
And when w're together, (Oh! soon may it be!)
The world may go kissing of comets for me!

3

The chair that Will sat in, I sit in the best;
The tobacco is sweetest which Willy hath blest;
And I never found out that my wine tasted ill
When a tear would drop in it, for thinking of Will.

4

And now on my windows October blows chilly,
I laugh at blue devils, & think of my Willy:
I think, that our friendship will not drop away
Like the leaves from the trees, or our locks when they're grey:
I think that old age shall not freeze us, until
He creeps with Death's warrant to me and my Will.

5

If I get to fifty—may Willy get too:
And we'll laugh, thrill, at all that grim sixty can do:
Old age?—let him do of what poets complain,
We'll thank him for making us children again;
Let him make us grey, gouty, blind, toothless, or silly,
Still old Ned shall be Ned—and old Willy be Willy!

6

We may both get so old that our senses expire
And leave us to doze half-alive by the fire:
Age may chill the warm hearts which I think so divine,
But what warmth it has, Willy, shall ever be thine!
And if our speech goes, we must pass the long hours
When the earth is laid bare with a Winter like our's,
Till death find us waiting him patiently still,
Willy looking at me, and I looking at Willy.[5]

In the letter, the second song, a nostalgic farewell to summer, mingles the sad and the merry:

1

Farewell to merry summertime—I hear the wintry gale
That bids me fill my pipe again, & tap the foaming ale.

The trees are dying fast without, & cheerless is the scene,
But tobacco leaves are sprouting, boys, and friendship's evergreen!

2

In summer, Friendship wanders out along the sunny plain,
But she swears she never feels so strong as o'er the fire again:
I hear the winds cry pipingly:—let's tackle to our cheer,
And drink a merry stirrup-cup to the departing year.

3

Old year full lusty hath thy youth, and summer manhood been,
Stretched out at ease beneath the sun, or in the forest green.
But now your pipe is cracked with age, & peevish you are grown.
While you chatter in the wood that you have starved to skin and bones!

4

No matter, friends—kind Nature blows some good with ev'ry gale:
And if October kills the year, he brews our nutbrown ale;
Then let's fill our glasses up, & drink his health with hearty minds
In ale as yellow as his leaves, & stronger than his winds![6]

FitzGerald's letters reveal a deep sentimental attachment to Thackeray; but they also indicate the reclusive element in FitzGerald's nature which made him always stay at a distance even from friends, as though fearing that proximity might bring reality too close and shatter the illusion that encompassed all of life. FitzGerald sounds a note of melancholy skepticism in the beginning of his letter:

Now, Thackeray, I lay you ten thousand pounds that you will be thoroughly disappointed when we come together—our letters have been so warm, that we shall expect each minute to contain a sentence like those in our letters. But in letters we are not always together: there are no blue devilish moments: one of us isn't kept waiting for the other: and above all in letters there is Expectation! I am thus foreboding because I have felt it—and put you on your guard very seriously about it, for the disappointment of such hopes has caused a flatness, then a disgust, and then a coldness betwixt many friends, I'm in mind."

In 1835 an important episode occurred in FitzGerald's life; he fell in love with a young girl, and seriously contemplated marriage. Writing to Thackeray from Wherstead on July 29, 1835, FitzGerald sought his advice:

And now, my dear Boy, do you be very sensible, and tell me one thing—think of it in your bed, and over your cigar, and for a whole week, and then send me word directly—shall I marry?—I vow to the Lord that I am upon the brink of saying "Miss—do you think you could marry me?" to a plain, sensible, girl, without a farthing! There now you have it—The pro's and con's are innumerable, and not to be consulted: for I have at last come to a conclusion in morals, which is this: that to certain persons of a doubting temper, and who search after much perfection, it is better to do a thing slap dash at once, and then conform themselves to it—I have always been very unmanly in my strivings to get things all compact and in good train—But to the question again—An't I in a bad way? Do you not see that I am far gone? I should be as poor as a rat, and live in a windy tenement in these parts, giving tea to acquaintances—I should lose all my bachelor trips to London and Cambridge, I should no more, oh never more!—have the merry chance of rattling over to see thee, old Will, in Paris, or at Constantinople, at my will—I should be tied down—these are to be thought of: but then I get a settled home, a good companion, and the other usual pro's that desperate people talk of—Now write me word quickly: lest the deed be done! to be sure, there is one thing: I think it is extremely probable that the girl wouldn't have me: for her parents are very strict in religion, and look upon me as something of a Pagan.

Though FitzGerald does not name the girl, she is believed to have been Elizabeth Charlesworth, the daughter of the Reverend John Charlesworth, the rector of Flowton near Ipswich, in Suffolk. Whether it was the opposition of the girl's parents, or FitzGerald's inability to obtain his mother's agreement to a financial settlement that would have enabled him to marry, the marriage did not take place.

Meanwhile, Thackeray had met and fallen in love with Isabella Shawe. Having procured himself a job as the correspondent in Paris for the *Constitutional and Public Ledger* at a salary of four hundred pounds a year, Thackeray married Isabella. But the *Ledger* failed, and Thackeray returned to London with his family and took up residence at 13 Great Coram Street. Thackeray's marriage did not separate the two friends, and FitzGerald was a frequent visitor at Thackeray's house. FitzGerald's sensitivity to the needs of others and his generosity soon endeared him to Isabella Thackeray, though she was sometimes nettled by Thackeray's spending too much time in the company of friends, who, being financially independent, did not have to earn their living as Thackeray did. In one of her letters to her mother-in-law, Mrs. Carmichael-Smyth, Isabella complains of FitzGerald and Thackeray's other friends who, she says, seemed unable to breathe without him. But she concedes quickly: "I must say that I believe Fitz would give W. his last shill^g and often thinks of what he can do that is obliging to me. I believe he has as much to suffer in other respects as any one. One sister mad and the second that he dearly loves dying of a complaint of the lungs. Then he has to grieve over the selfishness and utter heartlessness of his Mother, who does not seem to care if her children live or die."[7]

Thackeray's letters also show that FitzGerald helped him financially, not only during his college days, but also all through the years when Thackeray was struggling to provide for his family and to gain recognition as a writer. To FitzGerald's credit, his generosity never affected their relationship. Thackeray seems to have accepted FitzGerald's help as an act of friendship and love, that was not to be regarded as a burden of gratitude. In one of his letters, Thackeray shows himself deeply moved by his friend's generosity: "My dear friend and brother," he wrote in 1834 to FitzGerald, "May God grant that no time or circumstance ever should diminish this love between us; it seems to me a thing w^h one should cultivate & preserve as a virtue, as a kind of religion, of w^h it seems to have usurped the place & I hope to exercise this power. . . ."[8]

Thackeray's daughter, Anne Ritchie, speaks movingly of Fitz-Gerald's steadfast friendship during the dark days of Thackeray's life when his wife was ill and he himself in great financial difficulties. She recalls that FitzGerald's extraordinary goodness and generosity provided help and comfort to Thackeray: "Mr. FitzGerald gave him orders for drawings to distract him, and also to bring money into his empty purse; he wrote him long letters to cheer him, and shared his troubles with a liberal heart."[9]

The publication of *Vanity Fair* (1847–1848) finally established Thackeray's reputation as a novelist; he already had moved from his house in Great Coram Street where his friends from Cambridge—FitzGerald; Alfred and his brother Frederick Tennyson; John Kemble, the Anglo-Saxon scholar; and John Allen, later the Archdeacon of Salop—often gathered to talk, joke, sip brandy and water, and listen to Alfred Tennyson recite his poems. As Thackeray's reputation grew, his circle of friends expanded rapidly. Fashionable society lionized him, and he liked it. "He is become a great man I am told," FitzGerald wrote to Frederick Tennyson of Thackeray in a letter of May 4, 1848; he "goes to Holland House, and Devonshire House: and for some reason or other, will not write to me. But I am sure this is not because he is asked to Holland House." As Thackeray's social activities increased, he found less and less time for FitzGerald, who, in turn, shied away from high society. FitzGerald visited Thackeray once or twice at his house in Young Street, and once in Onslow Square, but the visits were short and at long intervals. The days of Great Coram Street were gone forever.

The old affection, however, was not entirely forgotten. In 1852, before leaving for a lecture tour in the United States, Thackeray wrote a touching letter to FitzGerald, his "dearest old friend," in which he appointed him his literary executor and asked him to publish his book of ballads if anything should happen to him. "And I should like my daughters to remember that you are the best and oldest friend their father ever had, and that you would act as such; as my literary executor, and so forth."[10] FitzGerald, who was greatly moved by this expression of his friend's "noble kindness," made a provision in his will bequeathing sums of money to Thackeray's two daughters. Informing Thackeray of this bequest, FitzGerald wrote, "You see you can owe me no thanks for giving what I can no longer use 'when I go down to the pit,' and it would be some satisfaction to me, and some diminution of the shame I felt on reading your letter, if 'after many days' your generous and constant friendship bore some sort of fruit, if not to yourself to those you are naturally anxious about."[11]

FitzGerald saw very little of Thackeray in the last years of his life, but he followed his friend's progress from his retreat in Suffolk and rejoiced unselfishly in Thackeray's success. On the night of Christmas, 1863, while FitzGerald was walking alone in the Seckford Almshouse Gardens, he was told by a friend of Thackeray's death. "I am surprised almost to find how much I am thinking of him," FitzGerald wrote to Samuel Laurence the painter, whom he later commissioned to make a copy of the portrait Laurence had done of Thackeray; "so little as I had seen him for the last ten years; not once for the last five. I had been told—by you, for one—that he was spoiled. I am glad therefore that I have scarce seen him since he was 'old Thackeray.' I keep reading his *Newcomes* of nights, and as it were hear him saying so much in it; and it seems to me as if he might be coming up my Stairs, and about to come (singing) into my Room, as in old Charlotte Street, etc., thirty years ago."[12]

FitzGerald at first thought very highly of Thackeray's *Pendennis* and *The Newcomes* and said that, compared to them, Fielding's works seemed coarse. As FitzGerald grew older, his literary tastes changed. "I cannot get on with books about the Daily Life which I find rather insufferable in practice about me," he confided to Samuel Laurence in a letter of December 30, 1875. "I never could read Miss Austen, nor (later) the famous George Eliot. Give me People, Places, and Things, which I don't and can't see; Antiquaries, Jeanie Deans, Dalgettys, etc. . . . . As to Thackeray's, they are terrible; I really look at them on the shelf, and am half afraid to touch them. He, you know, could go deeper into the Springs of Common Action than these Ladies: wonderful he is, but not Delightful, which one thirsts for as one gets old and dry."

The Tennyson brothers, Frederick, Charles, and Alfred were FitzGerald's contemporaries at Cambridge; however, FitzGerald's friendship with Alfred and then with Frederick did not start until after leaving Cambridge.[13] FitzGerald had heard Tennyson recite English ballads at Cambridge gatherings, and had admired the "Lady of Shalott" when it was circulated in manuscript form in 1832. Had FitzGerald so wished, he could have made Alfred's acquaintance in their college days, but not until 1835 is there any record of FitzGerald's meeting Tennyson. In April of that year their mutual friend Spedding invited FitzGerald and Tennyson to spend three weeks as his guests at his father's home, Mirehouse, by Bassenthwaite Lake in Cumberland. At Mirehouse, Tennyson showed FitzGerald the poems that he included later in the 1842 volume: the "Morte d'Arthur," "The Day-Dream," "The Lord of Burleigh," "Dora," and "The Gardener's Daughter." Tennyson recited the poems aloud to FitzGerald and Spedding one night "when all the house was mute." FitzGerald made a sketch of Tennyson which shows him reading. The face is hidden; only the back of the head and the broad shoulders can be seen, and a shock of untidy hair forms a halo and descends almost to his shoulders.

FitzGerald and Tennyson later went to Ambleside, where they

spent a week and where Spedding joined them for the last two days. Tennyson and FitzGerald went rowing on Lake Windermere; and FitzGerald recalled how, resting on their oars one calm day, and

looking into the lake quite unruffled and clear, Alfred quoted from the lines he had lately read us from the MS of "Morte d'Arthur" about the lonely lady of the lake and Excalibur—

> Nine years she wrought it, sitting in the deeps
> Upon the hidden bases of the hills.

Not Bad that, Fitz, is it?[14]

The stay at Mirehouse remained a memorable one for FitzGerald, and he looked back upon it always with great nostalgia. After James Spedding's death in 1881, FitzGerald wrote to Emily Tennyson, the poet's wife, on March 22, and referred to that month in May, 1835, "when the Daffodil was out in a field before the house, as I see them, though not in such force, owing to cold winds, before my window now. Does A. T. remember them?" In a letter of condolence to James Spedding's niece on July 31 of the same year, FitzGerald recalled how Spedding's father, a wealthy Cumberland farmer, had always wished that his son would turn his faculties to public affairs rather than to poetry; the poets he had seen in Cumberland only confirmed his low opinion of them:

Shelley, for one, at one time stalking about the mountains, with Pistols, and other such Vagaries. I do not think he was much an Admirer of Wordsworth (I don't know about Southey), and I well remember that when I was at Merehouse (as Miss Bristow would have us call it) with A. Tennyson in 1835, Mr. Spedding grudged his Son's giving up much time and thought to consultations about Morte d'Arthurs's, Lords of Burleighs, etc., which were then in MS. He more than once questioned me, who was sometimes present at the meetings: "Well, Mr. F., and what is it? Mr. Tennyson reads, and Jem criticizes:—is that it?" etc. This, while I might be playing Chess with dear Mrs. Spedding, in May, while the Daffodils were dancing outside the Hall door.

Though the dancing daffodils remained a part of FitzGerald's memory of the visit to Mirehouse, the weather seemed not to have proved as congenial to Alfred Tennyson who was described by his host as being "very gruff and unmanageable."[15] Tennyson's moodiness, his "almost personal dislike of the Present, whatever it may be," as Spedding put it, had some justification at this time of his life. Unlike FitzGerald and Spedding, who could look forward to a financially secure future, Tennyson had only uncertainty ahead of him. He had no money and no prospects of coming into any in the near future. He had deliberately chosen poetry as his life's work, and he knew that he had a long struggle ahead of him to establish his reputation as a poet. Adding to his unsettled state of mind was his habit of excessive smoking and his hypochondria, which FitzGerald charitably described as "an hereditary tenderness of nerve." Though Tennyson's "complaints and complainings" sometimes exhausted the patience of even FitzGerald, the latter was always ready to forgive him. FitzGerald saw him as "quite magnanimous, and noble natured, with no meanness or vanity or affectation of any kind whatever—but very perverse, according to the nature of his illness—So much for Poets, who, one must allow, are many of them a somewhat tetchy race—"[16]

FitzGerald's admiration for Tennyson extended beyond mere words of praise. Soon after their visit at Mirehouse, FitzGerald wrote to Tennyson offering him financial assistance:

I have heard you sometimes say that you are bound by the want of such and such a sum, and I vow to the Lord that I could not have a greater pleasure than transferring it to you on such occasions; I should not dare to say such a thing to a small man: but you are not a small man assuredly: and even if you do not make use of my offer, you will not be offended but put it to the right account. It is very difficult to persuade people in this world that one can part with a banknote without a pang. It is one of the most simple things I have ever done to talk thus to you, I believe: but here is an end; and be charitable to me.[17]

That Tennyson accepted this offer there is no doubt, for he had lost nearly all his money in 1844 and was reduced to grave financial straits. In a letter to FitzGerald this same year, Thomas Carlyle, the historian, repeated a remark made by Tennyson to him which shows that FitzGerald's help was unstinting. "He said of you," Carlyle wrote to FitzGerald, "that you were a man from whom one could accept money; which was a proud saying; which you ought to bless heaven for."[18] One of Carlyle's American friends, Charles Eliot Norton, records a conversation with Carlyle in 1873 in which the historian told him that, during the many years in Tennyson's poor days, FitzGerald used to give him three hundred pounds out of his annual income.[19]

The most important outcome of the early years of friendship between FitzGerald and Tennyson was the publication of the 1842 volume of poems by Tennyson. The poems had been in circulation in manuscript form for some time, and Tennyson's publisher, Edward Moxon, and Tennyson's friends, especially FitzGerald, continued to urge him to publish a collection of his works. But Tennyson hesitated. The criticism leveled at the 1832 volume of his poems had made Tennyson averse to submitting any work of his to print. When he found, however, that an American publisher was about to issue an unauthorized collection of his poems, Tennyson finally consented to Moxon's publishing an authorized version. Nonetheless, he so delayed going to the publisher's that FitzGerald finally carried him off "with violence" to Moxon, and the process of publication was started.

Tennyson's poetry was readied for the press in Spedding's rooms, the owner being away on a mission to the United States. The pages of the long "Butcher's Book," in which the poems were copied in Alfred Tennyson's very fine hand, were one by one torn out and sent to the printer. The pages were later consigned to the flames; but FitzGerald, who saved a few of them, presented the pages to Trinity College in 1861.

The 1842 volume of Tennyson's poems remained FitzGerald's favorite. He had predicted of Tennyson that, "with all his faults, he will publish such a volume as has not been published since the time of Keats: and which, once published, will never be suffered to die."[20] FitzGerald expected great things of Tennyson, for he thought him to be the oracle of his times. Always generous in praise and admiration for merit, especially of his friends, FitzGerald saw Tennyson's genius in a greatly magnified form. After the stay at Ambleside, FitzGerald confided in a letter to his friend John Allen:

I will say no more of Tennyson than that the more I have seen of him, the more cause I have to think him great. His little humours and grumpiness were so droll, that I was always laughing: and was often put in mind (strange to say) of my little unknown friend, Undine—I must however say, further, that I felt what Charles Lamb describes, a sense of depression at times from the overshadowing of a so much more lofty intellect than my own: this (though it may seem vain to say so) I never experienced before, though I have often been with much greater intellects: but I could not be mistaken in the universality of his mind; and perhaps I have received some benefit in the now more distinct consciousness of my dwarfishness.[21]

FitzGerald expected Tennyson to create a body of noble work which would elevate him to a place among the glorious triad of English literature: Chaucer, Shakespeare, and Milton. But Tennyson's later poems disappointed FitzGerald, though he found passages of beauty in all of them. FitzGerald did not care for *The Princess*, which he considered "a wretched waste of power at a time of life when a man ought to be doing his best."[22] *In Memoriam*, he said, was full of the finest things; but it was monotonous because it had "that air of being evolved by a Poetical Machine of the highest order." He thought that Tennyson had lost "the Impetus, the Lyrical oestrus," and he blamed the inactive life of the nineteenth century for this loss of power. Tennyson's mode of life, his addiction to tobacco, and his hypochondria were a constant disappointment to FitzGerald, whose ideal of a poet was modeled on the Greek heroes. After reading the fourth book of Thucydides, he wrote to a friend, "This was the way to write well; and this was the way to make literature respectable. Oh, Alfred Tennyson, could you but have the luck to be put to such employment! No man would do it better; a more heroic figure to head the defenders of his country could not be."[23]

FitzGerald shared the belief of many intellectuals of his time that England had lost the old virtues that had made her great. It hurt him greatly to see the countryside ravaged in the name of progress, and to know that the growing industrialization was breaking the bond between man and nature. He felt the need for a poet-philosopher to warn the race and save it from destruction. Tennyson's genius entitled him to assume such a role; but, to be able to sing heroic songs, FitzGerald thought that a man should also live a heroic life, or at least an active one, such as Shakespeare or Sir Walter Scott had done. To FitzGerald, Tennyson had adopted a mode of life the reverse of the heroic. "Tennyson is half-cured, or half-destroyed, from a water establishment: has gone to a new Doctor who gives him iron pills," FitzGerald wrote in 1848, "and altogether this really great man thinks more about his bowels and nerves than about the Laureate wreath he was born to inherit."[24] Tennyson's plan to write about King Arthur failed to arouse FitzGerald's enthusiasm. ". . . I believe the trumpet can wake Tennyson no longer to do great deeds," FitzGerald remarked in the same letter; "I may mistake and prove myself an owl; which I hope may be the case. But how are we to expect heroic poems from a valetudinary? I have told him he should fly from England and go among savages."

FitzGerald was aware that his criticism of Tennyson's poems would be attributed by some to envy; but Tennyson himself, and FitzGerald's close friends who knew him well, never doubted the sincerity of his motives or the integrity of his character. Those admirers of Tennyson who rendered him absolute and uncritical admiration, such as the poet's wife Emily Tennyson, and who, in FitzGerald's opinion, were responsible for the decline in the quality of Tennyson's verse, tended, in turn, to regard FitzGerald's criticism of Tennyson as a forgivable eccentricity. Emily Tennyson, who was fond of FitzGerald and corresponded with him, answered his letters to her husband; and, while admiring FitzGerald's nobility of temper and kindness of heart, she seemed to feel the pity of the initiated for those in the outer darkness: "It does not hurt me that dear old Fitz does not care—even for *In Memoriam* and *The Idylls of the King*," she wrote to Anne Thackeray Ritchie in 1889: "I feel it was a want in him that he *did not*, that is all, tho' naturally I would have all good and great people to understand them and delight in them. Aye and all good and little people too after their fashion."[25]

FitzGerald undoubtedly found amusement in his friends' opinions of his wayward tastes, but he was not deterred from speaking his mind. He told Hallam Tennyson, the poet's son, that the only song he liked in *The Princess* was "Blow, Bugle, Blow," adding, "That is one of Fitz's crotchets, and I am considered a great heretic because like Carlyle I gave up all hopes of him after *The Princess*."[26] He repeated in his notes sent to Hallam Tennyson a remark he had made before, that none of the songs in *The Princess* had "the old champagne flavour," but that "Alfred is the same magnanimous, kindly, delightful fellow as ever, uttering by far the finest prose-sayings of anyone." Hallam's acerbic comment on FitzGerald's criticism is that "nothing either by Thackeray or by my father met FitzGerald's approbation unless he had first seen it in manuscript."[27]

Though FitzGerald always maintained that Tennyson's later poems were mediocre, he still regarded Tennyson as a poet of great stature, far above the Pre-Raphaelites or Robert Browning, whose style he dubbed the Gargoyle School of Poetry. Perhaps FitzGerald's affection for Tennyson led him to expect more from him than he would have otherwise, just as FitzGerald's extreme modesty prevented him from seeing any merit in his own literary efforts. "Had I Alfred's voice," he wrote to Frederick Tennyson in December, 1851, "I would not have mumbled for years over 'In Memoriam' and the 'Princess.' . . . What can 'In Memoriam' do but make us all sentimental?"

FitzGerald's criticism of Tennyson's poems did not affect their relationship, and the two retained their affection for each other. After the poet's marriage, FitzGerald continued to visit the Tennysons occasionally. He went to see them and the new baby at Seaford, and spent a week with the Tennysons on the Isle of Wight in the summer of 1854. FitzGerald, who was then absorbed in the study of Persian, tried to get Tennyson to learn Persian; but the dots and strokes of the Persian characters bothered Tennyson's eyes, and he abandoned the study of the language.

In later years, FitzGerald no longer visited his friends, and kept in touch with most of them by letters only. Although the Tennysons invited him repeatedly to the Isle of Wight, the hustle and bustle surrounding the now famous poet laureate kept FitzGerald away. In 1876, however, the two friends met again when Tennyson, accompanied by his son Hallam, was touring Norfolk and stopped at Woodbridge to see FitzGerald. Twenty years had passed since the two had met, but it seemed to FitzGerald that Tennyson had not changed much, except for his "fallen locks." It surprised FitzGerald that they "fell at once into the old Humour, as if we had only been parted twenty Days instead of so many Years. I suppose this is a Sign of Age—not altogether desirable. But so it was. He stayed two Days, and we went over the same old grounds of Debate, told some of the old Stories, and all was well. I suppose I may never see him again: and so I suppose we both thought as the Rail carried him off: and each returned to his ways as if scarcely diverted from them."[28] Tennyson and his son did not stay at FitzGerald's house, Little Grange, as it was being painted, but were lodged at the local inn at their host's expense. They spent a day with FitzGerald in his garden, sitting under the roses in the sunlight. Tennyson recalled the scene in his lines "To E. FitzGerald" which were prefixed to his *Tiresias:*

Old Fitz, who from your suburb grange,
    Where once I tarried for a while,
Glance at the wheeling orb of change,
    And greet it with a kindly smile;
Whom yet I see as there you sit
    Beneath your sheltering garden-tree,
And watch your doves about you flit,
    And plant on shoulder, hand, and knee,
Or on your head their rosy feet,
    As if they knew your diet spares
Whatever moved in that full sheet
    Let down to Peter at his prayers;
Who live on milk, and meal, and grass;
    And once for ten long weeks I tried
Your table of Pythagoras,
    And seemed at first 'a thing enskied,'
As Shakespeare has it, airy-light
    To float above the ways of men,
Then fell from that half-spiritual height
    Chill'd, till I tasted flesh again
One night when earth was winter-black,
    And all the heavens flash'd in frost;
And on me, half-asleep, came back
    That wholesome heat the blood had lost,
And set me climbing icy capes
    And glaciers, over which there roll'd
To meet me long-arm'd vines with grapes
    Of Eschol hugeness; for the cold
Without, and warmth within me, wrought
    To mould the dream; but none can say
That Lenten fare makes Lenten thought
    Who reads your golden Eastern lay,
Than which I know no version done
    In English more divinely well;
A planet equal to the sun
    Which cast it, that large infidel
Your Omar; and your Omar drew
    Full-handed plaudits from our best
In modern letters, and from two,
    Old friends outvaluing all the rest,
Two voices heard on earth no more;
    But we old friends are still alive,
And I am nearing seventy-four,
    While you have touch'd at seventy-five,

And so I send a birthday line
    Of greeting; and my son, who dipt
In some forgotten book of mine
    With sallow scraps of manuscript,
And dating many a year ago,
    Has hit on this, which you will take,
My Fitz, and welcome, as I know,
    Less for its own than for the sake
Of one recalling gracious times,
    When, in our younger London days,
You found some merit in my rhymes,
    And I more pleasure in your praise.

But FitzGerald did not live to see this tribute from the poet
laureate. *Tiresias* was published after FitzGerald's death; before it
went to press, Tennyson added an epilogue:

"One height and one far-shining fire!"
    And while I fancied that my friend
For this brief idyll would require
    A less diffuse and opulent end,
And would defend his judgment well,
    If I should deem it over nice—
The tolling of his funeral bell
    Broke on my Pagan Paradise,
And mixt the dream of classic times,
    And all the phantoms of the dream,
With present grief, and made the rhymes,
    That miss'd his living welcome, seem
Like would-be guests an hour too late,
    Who down the highway moving on
With easy laughter find the gate
    Is bolted and the master gone.
Gone into darkness, that full light
    Of friendship! past, in sleep, away
By night, into the deeper night!
    The deeper night? A clearer day
Than our poor twilight dawn on earth—
    If night, what barren toil to be!
What life, so maim'd by night, were worth
    Our living out? Not mine to me
Remembering all the golden hours
    Now silent, and so many dead,
And him the last; and laying flowers,

> This wreath, above his honor'd head,
> And praying that, when I from hence
> Shall fade with him into the unknown,
> My close of earth's expperience
> May prove as peaceful as his own.

One name remains to be added to this short account of FitzGerald's famous friends—that of Thomas Carlyle, whom Fitz-Gerald met in 1842 through Samuel Laurence, the painter. FitzGerald was already familiar with Carlyle's books, which were creating a great deal of controversy among the intellectuals. FitzGerald counted himself among those who praised rather than abused the Scotsman, but he did not always subscribe to Carlyle's opinions. At the time that FitzGerald became acquainted with the historian, he was engaged in writing the life of Oliver Cromwell and was keenly interested in finding the exact location of the Battle of Naseby. FitzGerald's parents owned the land where the battle had taken place, and FitzGerald's father had erected an obelisk on high ground. The obelisk, however, was at some distance from the actual site of the battle, a fact of which Carlyle was not aware. FitzGerald, who pointed out the mistake, went to a great deal of trouble and expense to locate for Carlyle the exact area where the main battle had taken place; thus began a deep and lasting friendship between the two men.

FizGerald saw a great deal of Carlyle during the 1840s when he visited London frequently to see his friends, to attend the theaters, and to visit the art galleries. Carlyle was then living at No. 5 Cheyne Row, and FitzGerald spent many a pleasant evening there. He describes one such occasion in a letter of April 11, 1844, to his Quaker friend, Bernard Barton:

I smoked a pipe with Carlyle yesterday. We ascended from his dining room carrying pipes and tobacco up through two stories of his house, and got into a little dressing room near the roof: there we sat down: the window was open and looked out on nursery gardens, their almond trees in bloom, and beyond, bare walls of houses, and over these, roofs and chimneys, and roofs and chimneys, and here and there a steeple, and whole London crowned with darkness gathering behind like the illimitable resources of a dream. I tried to persuade him to leave the accursed den, and he wished—but—but—perhaps he didn't wish on the whole.

Sometimes the evening did not go so well. The prophet would be in a declamatory mood, and would lecture for hours on end until the guests were very glad to get away. "I met C. last night at Tennyson's," FitzGerald wrote to Barton of one such evening, "and they two discussed the merits of this world, and the next, till I wished myself out of *this*, at any rate."[29] FitzGerald did not see any point to Carlyle's denunciations: "Carlyle gets more wild, savage, and unreasonable every day," he added in the same letter; "and, I do believe, will turn mad. 'What is the use of ever so many rows of stupid, fetid, animals in cauliflower wigs—and clean lawn sleeves—calling themselves Bishops—Bishops, I say, of the Devil—not of God—obscene creatures parading between men's eyes, and the eternal light of Heaven,' &c. &c. This, with much abstruser nonconformity for 2 whole hours!—and even as it was yesterday, so shall it be to-morrow, and the day after that—in saecula saeculorum!—" But if FitzGerald tired sometimes of Carlyle's fulminations, his whimsical humor did not desert him for long. "I spent one evening with Carlyle," he wrote to Barton on July 11, 1845," but was very dull somehow, and delighted to get out into the street: and Carlyle was rather amazed to see me polka down the pavement—He shut his street door—to which he always accompanied you—with a kind of groan."

For his part, Carlyle had genuine affection for FitzGerald. "A modest, shy, studious man, of much character, much loved by Thackeray and others," Carlyle described him once to Norton.[30] Carlyle even overcame his aversion to travel to visit FitzGerald in Suffolk, staying at Farlingay farm as FitzGerald's guest. In later years, when FitzGerald's visits to London became infrequent, he kept his friendship with Carlyle alive by correspondence. "Thanks for your friendly human letter; which gave us much entertainment in the reading (at breakfast time the other day), and is still pleasant to think of," Carlyle once wrote in reply to FitzGerald. "One gets so many *in*human letters, ovine, bovine, porcine, etc., etc.: I wish you would write a little oftener; when the beneficent Daimon suggests, fail not to lend an ear to him."[31] In 1880, when FitzGerald was in London on business, he was "half tempted to jump into a Bus and just leave my name at Carlyle's Door." But he did not. Carlyle died in February, 1881. Two years later, when FitzGerald was in London, he went to see Carlyle's statue on the Chelsea Embankment;

he thought it very good, though looking somewhat small and ill set off by its dingy surroundings. He went to Cheyne Row, which he had not seen for twenty-five years. No. 5, where he had spent many a pleasant evening, was "all neglected, unswept, ungarnished, uninhabited . . ." and marked "To Let."[32]

If the literary fame of FitzGerald's three friends, Thackeray, Tennyson, and Carlyle is important to students of literature, it should be remembered that their success meant very little to FitzGerald as far as his affection for them was concerned. Devoid of both ambition and envy, FitzGerald could rejoice in the prosperity of his friends. But, since crowds repelled him, he withdrew rather than join the throng of adulators around Thackeray and Tennyson. Moreover, FitzGerald had his own standards of greatness which were different from those of others. As great a genius in his way as Thackeray or Tennyson, he made no effort to seek fame; instead, he deliberately eschewed recognition, published his translations anonymously, and sedulously avoided publicity. His biographers have pitied him for his lack of purpose, criticized him for his indolence, and attributed his lack of ambition to the absence of pecuniary need which spurred Thackeray and Tennyson to fame.

FitzGerald's own friends were sometimes dismayed by his indifference to recognition and fame. His friend Bernard Barton, who was an indefatigable poet and writer, tried to get FitzGerald to publish more, especially poetry, but FitzGerald answered him that, "as to my doing anything else in that way, I know that I could write volume after volume as well as others of the mob of gentlemen who write with ease: but I think unless a man can do better, he had best not do at all; I have not the strong inward call, nor cruel-sweet pangs of parturition, that prove the birth of anything bigger than a mouse."[33] Another explanation may also be found in FitzGerald's early verses, "The Meadows in Spring," "Chronomoros," and "Bredfield Hall," which reveal his overwhelming sense of the transient nature of life, and a melancholy that is unusual in a man in the prime of life. FitzGerald's sensitive nature could not take decay and death in stride as his friends did. Having seen through the outer trappings of life to its essential sadness, FitzGerald could not beguile himself with the thought that success makes all worthwhile. He had the makings of a mystic in him, but he was also a man of the nineteenth century when science brought skepticism along with knowledge. FitzGerald had too keen an eye for the absurdities of human nature to have unquestioning faith in any belief. He was unable to muster in himself an earnestness of purpose; because he perceived life to be a short illusion, purpose had no meaning. His was a dilemma that has faced man since he first learned to think and to deduce. The same doubts troubled another poet centuries ago, as FitzGerald would find when he discovered the quatrains of Omar Khayyam.

CHAPTER 2

Early Works

I   *"The Meadows in Spring,"* Euphranor, *and* Polonius

FITZGERALD published his first poem when he was twenty-two years of age. Entitled "The Meadows in Spring," the poem appeared by an odd chance in two periodicals within the space of a few months: in William Hone's *Year Book* of April 30, 1831, and in the *Athenaeum* of July 9, 1831. The poem, which was anonymous, may have been submitted first to the *Athenaeum*, which delayed in publishing it; FitzGerald, taking its silence for rejection, probably sent the poem to Hone's *Year Book*. In both periodicals, the poem was accompanied by the author's letter. In his note to the *Athenaeum*, the author stated, "These verses are something in the old style, but not the worse for that: not that I mean to call them good: but I am sure that they would not have been better, if dressed up in the newest Montgomery fashion. If they are fitted for your paper, you are welcome to them."

The *Athenaeum* was not only apologetic about its tardiness, but was also full of praise for the anonymous poet. The excellence of the poem led the editor to believe that it was one of Charles Lamb's compositions, and he hinted as much in his reply to the poet's letter published with the poem: "They are fitted for any paper, and most welcome to us. The writer must not imagine that the delay in their appearance was occasioned by any doubt. . . . His verses are not, indeed, in the Montgomery style, or the latest fashion—they are not all glare and glitter, patch and paint, and meretricious ornament— they are deep in feeling, and sweet in harmony; but we must not write commendations even on contributors. We have a suspicion that we could name the writer—if so, we are sure his name would grace our pages as much as his verses."

Charles Lamb, who had seen "The Meadows in Spring" in the

Year Book for April and who realized that the *Athenaeum* believed him to be the author, wrote to his publisher Edward Moxon: "The Athenaeum has been hoaxed with some exquisite poetry, that was, two or three months ago, in Hone's Book. . . . The poem I mean is in Hone's Book as far back as April. I do not know who wrote it; but 'tis a poem I envy—*that* and Montgomery's "Last Man": I envy the writers because I feel I could have done something like them."[1]

"The Meadows in Spring" is written in a fine lyrical style, and it is redolent with FitzGerald's bittersweet view of life:

> 'Tis a dull sight
>   To see the year dying,
> When the winter winds
>   Set the yellow woods sighing:
>   Sighing, oh! sighing.
>
> When such a time cometh,
>   I do retire
> Into an old room
>   Beside a bright fire:
>   Oh, pile a bright fire!
>
> And there I sit
>   Reading old things,
> Of knights and lorn damsels,
>   While the wind sings—
>   Oh, drearily sings!
>
> I never look out
>   Nor attend to the blast;
> For all to be seen
>   Is the leaves falling fast:
>   Falling, falling!
>
> But close at the hearth,
>   Like a cricket, sit I.
> Reading of summer
>   And chivalry—
>   Gallant chivalry!
>
> Then with an old friend
>   I talk of our youth—
> How 'twas gladsome, but often

Foolish, forsooth:
But gladsome, gladsome!

Or to get merry
We sing some old rhyme,
That made the wood ring again
In summer time—
Sweet summer time!

Then go we to smoking
Silent and snug
Nought passes between us,
Save a brown jug—
Sometimes!

And sometimes a tear
Will rise in each eye,
Seeing the two old friends
So merrily—
So merrily!

And ere to bed
Go we, go we,
Down on the ashes
We kneel on the knee,
Praying together!

Thus, then, live I,
Till, 'mid all the gloom,
By heaven! the bold sun
Is with me in the room,
Shining, shining!

Then the clouds part,
Swallows soaring between;
The spring is alive,
And the meadows are green!

I jump up, like mad,
Break the old pipe in twain,
And away to the meadows,
The meadows again!

The enthuiastic reception of FitzGerald's first poem should have augured well for the future of FitzGerald's literary career; but, ironically, "The Meadows in Spring" was the only one of his works published in an influential periodical. Except for a few minor pieces, FitzGerald's poems, including the *Rubáiyát*, were rejected by journals and ignored by critics. His translations and prose works were printed by himself; and all, except one, were published anonymously.

FitzGerald's first prose work, *Euphranor: A Dialogue on Youth*, was printed in 1851 by Charles Childs of Bungay, a publisher who was recommended to FitzGerald by Thomas Carlyle. *Euphranor* was the result of FitzGerald's conviction that the English system of education was in great need of reform. He disliked the rigorous discipline to which children were subjected, and he deplored the lack of attention to a child's physical well-being and to the development of his total personality. English schools, in FitzGerald's opinion, did not prepare a youth for participation in the affairs of his community, and the universities served him no better in this regard. Education, as the ancient Greeks understood it, was not imparted in the schools and universities of England. A young man obtained a degree, but he acquired none of the accomplishments that an earlier age had regarded as necessary to a well-rounded, balanced education, such as skill in horsemanship and sports. In *Euphranor*, FitzGerald shows how the goals of English education could be changed to conform to the ideals of chivalry and to the precepts of philosophers.

FitzGerald had started *Euphranor* in 1846, but it was not until 1850 when a visit to Cambridge revived his interest in the subject of education that he completed the manuscript and sent it to the printer's. The dialogue, which follows the Platonic form, is carried on by four participants: Euphranor, an intelligent student of great promise; Lexilogus, a hard-working honors student whose sole ambition is to make good grades in the examinations; Lycion, an intelligent but indolent undergraduate whose predominant interest is the pursuit of pleasure; and the Doctor, who assumes the role of the narrator. The fifth participant is Phidippus, who is acquainted with the classics but is not a scholar, who is a man of action, an accomplished horseman, and blessed with good humor and a becoming modesty. FitzGerald modeled Phidippus after a friend whom he admired greatly, William Kenworthy Browne of Bedford. Browne, a captain in the militia and a skillful rider and sportsman, was also interested in art and literature but not to the extent that thought overshadowed capacity for action. He was, in FitzGerald's opinion, the example of a well-balanced personality; for he combined intellectual refinement with athletic prowess. The ideal Briton, as FitzGerald described him in *Euphranor*, "was sufficiently qualified, not only to shoot the Pheasant and hunt the Fox, but even to sit on the Bench of Magistrates—or even of Parliament—not unprovided with a quotation or two from Horace or Virgil." Browne, or Phidippus, was thus a man much better equipped than FitzGerald himself to live a successful and active life; and the creation of a balanced personality such as Browne's, FitzGerald thought, should be the aim of English schools.

Lexilogus and Lycion, on the other hand, represent the undesirable types who were generally found in the university system. Lycion idles his time away, and Lexilogus is so obsessed with examinations and grades that he remains ignorant of everything but the prescribed curriculum. At one point he confesses that he has not read Chaucer, a cardinal sin in the eyes of FitzGerald to whom Chaucer's works were the glory of the English language. When FitzGerald started writing the dialogue, he intended to call the work "Phidippus" after its hero; but, as the book progressed, Euphranor emerged as the most articulate figure, with Phidippus appearing only toward the end of the book. Thus, in its final form, the dialogue was named after the chief speaker; but Phidippus remained the hero-image.

Euphranor starts on a brisk and light note: "During the time of my pretending to practice medicine at Cambridge, I was aroused one fine forenoon of May, by the sound of some one running up my staircase, three or four steps at a time; then, directly, a smart rapping at the door; and, before I could say 'come in,' Euphranor had opened it, and, coming up to me, seized my arm with his usual eagerness, and told me I must go out with him." FitzGerald begins his dialogue on a day in May in the English countryside after the custom of the Middle English writers and of his own beloved Chaucer to whom he pays tribute later in the dialogue: "And look at dear old Chaucer himself . . . how the fresh air of the Kent hills, over which he rode four hundred years ago, breathes in his verses still. They have a perfume like fine old hay, that will not lose its sweetness, having been cut and carried so fresh. All his poetry bespeaks a man of sound mind and body."

Throughout the dialogue, FitzGerald dwells on the theme of a sound mind in a sound body. Using Kenelm Digby's discussion of chivalry as a starting point, FitzGerald shows how the ideals of chivalry should be applied to the training and education of young men from the time they are born until they are independent adults. His imaginary Sir Launcelot would be subject to as few restrictions as possible; he would be reared in familiarity with nature and with animals, especially the horse and the dog, both of which, FitzGerald points out, have traditionally embodied the virtues of devotion and courage. Such a child would be

A jolly little fellow, with rosy cheeks, and a clear eye, with just a little mischief in it at times: passionate, perhaps, and (even with his sisters) apt to try right by might; but generous, easily pacified, easily repentant, and ready to confess his faults; rather rebellious against women's domination, and against all the wraps and gruels they force upon him; but fond of mother, and of good old nurse; glad to begin and end each day with a prayer and a little hymn at their knees. Decidedly fonder of play than of books; rather too fond, it is supposed, of the stable, and of Will and Tom there; but submitting, after a little contest, to learn a little day by day from books which lead his mind towards hope, affection, generosity, and piety.

At seven years of age, Launcelot would be enrolled in school; but he would not be subjected to the curriculum usually followed in the schools of his day, especially the lesser known ones, which required as much as twelve hours of indoor study, and allowed only two hours for recreation that consisted of a walk with the schoolmaster. FitzGerald would reduce greatly the number of hours spent by children in the classroom, would let them enjoy the outdoors instead, and allow them to participate in sports, preferably those that carried some danger with them. High among the accomplishments FitzGerald considers desirable in a young man is horseback riding, and it would be included in the school curriculum wherever possible, as was the custom, he points out, in some European schools.

FitzGerald frequently refers to Fellenberg's school in Germany where many of the reforms he advocates had already been introduced, in order to show that his proposals were not merely the impractical suggestions of an idealist, but were reforms that had proved both possible and successful. But, staunch Englishman that he is, FitzGerald makes it clear that he is not in favor of sending young men to Germany for their schooling; he adheres to "old dogmas about an Englishman being brought up in England, imbibing English air and English associations into his very nature from the first." He declares, "I am for growing up by the Thames under Windsor Castle, rather than by the Rhine under Heidelberg."

FitzGerald is critical of the methods of education followed in many of the smaller schools, which had none of the traditions of the larger and older schools to recommend them: ". . . My dear Euphranor, you cannot imagine the pusillanimous, sordid, soul-and-body stunting methods of some of these, which, if English good sense did not explode just before it was too late, (as English good sense has somehow a knack of doing,) would ruin the middle-class Chivalry of England altogether." The typical young man who emerged from these schools was the antithesis of the chivalric: "The last I heard of him was, that after a most unimpeachable progress through school and college, getting all the prizes, he was going off to some new German baths covered with boils and blotches; or, at the Old Bailey, laying his hand on that part of his coat under which the heart is supposed to beat, and calling God to witness the innocence of a murderer who had already confessed his crime to him." Quite different is the progress of FitzGerald's ideal young man who will not conform to the suffocating discipline of school and who refuses to fit into the conventional mold:

It is only one of Nature's "best earthly mould," with the spirit of her chivalry strong in his blood, who kicks over the traces, throws the whole "very eligible establishment" into disorder, and rouses the whole dastard soul of Skythrops into a meagre attitude of expulsion, however unwilling he may be to part with any victim who pays. But "he must go—nothing can be done with him—" He goes: he is sent to sea—rolls and tosses over the world,—comes back a good-humoured, active, lively, sun-burnt fellow, with tobacco and cheroots for his old Dad; some silks for mother and sisters; a parrot for old aunt Deborah; a bamboo, which he says he would give old Skythrops but for fear he should lick the boys with it. So he travels, and returns, and travels again, has at last scraped a little money together; marries a good-humoured girl who has even less world's wealth than himself; nay, I believe he had married her long before he was even as rich as he is;—has a large family of children as healthy as himself—the more the merrier, he says; and so whistles through and over the ups and downs of life.

FitzGerald's ideal young man and his pursuits bear little resemblance to FitzGerald's own life. The whole of *Euphranor,* with its emphasis on action and daring rather than inactive contemplation, is a refutation of what FitzGerald considered his own defective upbringing—a Hamlet-like castigation of his own imagined weaknesses. FitzGerald emphasizes action, insisting that even poets should be men of the world, as were the truly great ones such as Homer, Aeschylus, Chaucer, Shakespeare, and Scott. FitzGerald's ideal poet would have, in addition to genius, a strong and active body capable of endurance and exposure, that would enable the poet to be with nature "in all her humours, and to penetrate all her mysteries—of calm, of storm, land and sea, day and night, mountain or forest."

In the second edition of *Euphranor,* published in 1855, FitzGerald included Tennyson in his roster of great poets, though he did not name him:

Really the only Great Poet I had seen was of great Mould and Muscle; having used as a Boy, I was told, to be out upon the Hills Night after Night, with Shepherd and Sheep, whose individual Faces and Voices he not only grew to distinguish, but, both in Heaven above and Earth beneath, many of those uncertain phenomena of Night—the sound of falling Weirs and creeping Brooks, and Copses muttering to themselves afar off, perhaps the yet more impossible Sea—all inaudible to the Ear of Day; and not only the "Consistory of the Nightly Stars," and their gradual Dispersion by the Dawn, but also certain unsurmised Apparitions of the Northern Aurora, by some shy Glimpses of which silverying some low-lying Horizon Cloud in their customary quarter of the Heavens, scarce any Winter—no, nor even Summer—Night, he said, was utterly unvisited.

In the third edition of *Euphranor,* which FitzGerald published in 1882, he lengthened the passage on Tennyson to include an anecdote about him describing how, finding himself beside the river Doon, he "broke into a passion of tears—of tears which, during a pretty long and intimate intercourse, I had never seen glisten in his eye but once, when reading Virgil—'dear old Virgil,' as he call'd him—together: and then of the burning of Troy in the Second Aeneid—whether moved by the catastrophe's self, or the majesty of the Verse it is told in—or, as before, scarce knowing why." He also added another recollection of Tennyson:

"Nevertheless," said Euphranor, "I have heard tell of another Poet's saying that he knew of no human outlook so solemn as that from an Infant's Eyes; and how it was from those of his own he learn'd that those of the Divine Child in Raffaelle's Sistine Madonna were not over-charged with expression, as he had previously thought they might be."

"I think," I said, "you must have heard of that from me, who certainly did hear something like it from the Poet himself, who used to let fall—not lay down—the word that settled the question, aesthetic or other, which others hammer'd after in vain. Yes; that was on occasion, I think, of having watch'd his Child one morning *worshipping the Sunbeam on the Bed-post. . . .'* "

In a letter to Hallam Tennyson of May 28, 1882, FitzGerald referred to these two passages and asked Hallam to find out if his father disapproved of their being included in the third edition of *Euphranor:* "He did not object, so far as I know, to what I said of him, though not by name, in a former Edition; but there is more of him in this, though still not by name, nor, as you see, intended for Publication. All of this you can read to him, if you please, at pp. 25 and 56. I do not ask him to say that he approves of what is said, or meant to be said, in his honour; and I only ask you to tell me if he disapproves of its going any further." FitzGerald seemed to have had a premonition of his own death: "I really did, and do, wish my first, which is also my last, little work to record, for a few years at least, my love and admiration of that dear old Fellow, my old Friend." Tennyson must not have objected to the two passages, for they were included in the last edition of *Euphranor.*

Though a small book of eighty-one pages when it first appeared, *Euphranor* reveals the great care and artistry that FitzGerald devoted to all of his literary creations. But the work lacks the spontaneity and humor that are the outstanding traits of FitzGerald's style. FitzGerald himself was conscious of the difficulty of writing dialectic in the form of natural conversation, and he confessed that the dialogue appeared affected in places. To the reader, a major shortcoming of *Euphranor* is that the participants fail to come alive; they remain throughout stereotyped mouthpieces for FitzGerald's views. Lexilogus contributes little to the dialogue other than representing the bookish type of student; and Phidippus, for all his admirable qualities, arrives only toward the end of the book and makes little impression upon the reader. The only character in the dialogue who displays any spark of individuality is Lycion, whose whimsical remarks and eloquent gestures provide a relief from Euphranor's earnest arguments. One cannot help seeing FitzGerald's wry humor in Lycion's irreverent statements and his sly digs at the pomposity of Euphranor and the Doctor. At one point, after listening to the serious discussion of the chivalric virtues that is carried on at great

length by Euphranor and the Doctor, Lycion interjects his own
observation:

"I am told the old knights were really great blackguards," said Lycion,
turning his cigar in his mouth and glancing at his antagonist, "with all the
pretences of fighting for religion, distressed damsels, and so on."

"Come Lycion," said I, "you must not abuse them, you, whose pedigree
links you through Agincourt and Crecy, almost up to the times of King
Arthur."

"O yes, King Arthur and his round table, and the seven champions; and
pray do not forget Don Quixote. He is one of your heroes, is he not,
Euphranor?"

Euphranor declared that Don Quixote was a man of truly chivalric
soul—only—

"Only that he was mad," interrupted Lycion," and mistook windmills for
giants. And I doubt if King Arthur's giants, ogres, and dragons were half so
substantial as windmills."

"Perhaps Digby would tell us," said I, who saw Euphranor's wrath rising,
"that there can be no want of dragons and ogres while oppression and
misery are to be found in the world."

Though Lycion's part is small, he manages to focus a great deal of
attention on himself; and the reader wishes that FitzGerald had
developed him more fully. Perhaps FitzGerald did not want Lycion
to overshadow the hero and did not desire too much humor in a
serious work; for whatever reason, Lycion's part remained small in
the later editions.

Though *Euphranor* did not accomplish the purpose for which it
was written—the reform of the English system of education—the
book was not entirely ignored. Favorable reviews appeared in *The
Examiner* of February 8, 1851, and in the *Westminster Review*, by
FitzGerald's friends James Spedding and E. B. Cowell; other re-
viewers in *The Gentleman's Magazine*, *The Spectator*, and *The
Literary Gazette* also praised *Euphranor* for its elegant style. Tennyson declared that the description of the boat race at the end of the
book was one of the best pieces of prose in the English language.
FitzGerald himself always remained fond of the little book he called
"a pretty specimen of 'chisell'd Cherry-stone.' " In the two later
editions, FitzGerald made additions and deletions, but he left un-
touched the concluding passage with its lyrical description of the
boat race:

Shortly after this, the rest of us agreed it was time to be gone. We walked along the fields past the church, crossed the boat-house ferry, and mingled with the crowd upon the opposite bank. Townsmen and Gownsmen, with the laced Fellow-commoner sprinkled among them here and there— reading men and sporting men—Fellows, and even Masters of Colleges, not indifferent to the prowess of their respective crews—all these, conversing on all topics, from the slang in Bell's Life to the last new German Revelation, and moving in ever-changing groups down the banks, where, at the farthest visible bend of the river, was a little knot of ladies gathered up on a green knoll, faced and illuminated by the beams of the setting sun. Beyond which point was heard at length some indistinct shouting, which gradually increased, until "They are off—they are coming," suspended other conversation among ourselves: and suddenly the head of the first boat turned the corner, and then another close upon it, and then a third; the crews pulling with all their might, but in perfect rhythm and order; and the crews upon the bank turning round to follow along with them, cheering, "Bravo, St. John's," "Go it, Trinity," and waving hats and caps—the high crest and blowing forelock of Phidippus's mare, and he himself shouting encouragement to his crew, conspicuous over all—until, the boats reaching us, we also were caught up in the returning tide of spectators, and hurried back toward the boat-house; where we arrived just in time to see the ensign of Trinity lowered from its pride of place, and the eagle of St. John's soaring there instead. Then, waiting a while to hear how it was the winner had won, and the loser had lost, and watching Phidippus engaged in eager conversation with his defeated brethren, I took Euphranor and Lexilogus, one under each arm, (Lycion having strayed into better company elsewhere) and walked home with them across the meadow that lies between the river and the town, whither the dusky groups of gownsmen were evaporating, while twilight gathered over all, and the nightingale began to be heard among the flowering Chestnuts of Jesus.

FitzGerald drew upon his wide reading in the classics, in English, and Continental literature to embellish *Euphranor* with a wealth of quotations. His next book, published in 1852, was a selection of proverbs and aphorisms that was aptly titled, *Polonius: a Collection of Wise Saws and Modern Instances.* He chose quotations from more than a hundred classical, English, and Continental authors; but he also included a few from the Persian mystic and poet, Jelaluddin Rumi. To save the collection from becoming stilted and lifeless, he interspersed quotations with extracts from conversations of friends, his own comments, and fables and old proverbs, the last of which he regarded as "historical indexes of the nation that originates or retains them. . . ." The preface, which in itself is an exercise in the skillful use of quotations, starts with the author's apology: "Few books are duller than books of Aphorisms and Apophthegms. A Jest-book is, proverbially, no joke; a Wit-book, perhaps, worse; but dullest of all, probably, is the Moral-book, which this little volume pretends to be." The elegant essay that follows disproves FitzGererald's opening statement; for precepts and epigrams are so cleverly sewn into the body of the fabric that not a seam is left showing, and the interest of the reader is never allowed to flag.

The largest number of quotations in *Polonius* are from Sir Francis Bacon whose apophthegms. FitzGerald thought, were "the best collection of many men's sayings; the greatest variety of wisdom, good sense, wit, humour, and even simple naïvete, (as one must call it for want of a native word,) all told in a style whose dignity and antiquity (together with perhaps our secret consciousness of the gravity and even tragic greatness of the narrator) add a particular humour to the lighter stories."

Knowledge and Half-Knowledge

Knowledge is nothing but a representation of truth—for the truth of being and the truth of knowing are one, differing no more than the direct beam and the beam reflected.

Bacon

The quick decision of one who sees half the truth.

Next to Bacon, Carlyle seems to be FitzGerald's favorite philosopher; but not many contemporaries appear in the collection. The only others included besides Carlyle are Cardinal Newman, Tennyson, and Thackeray. FitzGerald does a great deal of his garnering from the English theologians and philosophers of the sixteenth, seventeenth, and eighteenth centuries, many of whom, he thought, were overlooked in popular anthologies.

FitzGerald arranges each quotation under a separate heading. Sometimes, to illustrate how a subject, elaborated in a passage, has been summarized neatly in a sentence, he inserts a proverb at the beginning or the end of the selection. He shows a particular fondness for English adages. "Our English Proverbs," he explains in the preface, "abound with good sense, energy, and courage, as compactly expressed as may be; making them properly enough the

ready money of a people more apt to act than talk." He occasionally
uses an English saying, together with passages on the same subject
from philosophers of widely differing backgrounds, such as in the
following selections from La Rochefoucald, Carlyle, and Jelaluddin
Rumi; all are elaborating on the subject set forth in the English proverb: "An empty skull is the Devil's Workshop":

Idleness

La paresse, toute languissante qu'elle est, ne laisse pas d'en être souvent
la maîtresse; elle usupe sur tous les desseins et sur toutes les actions de la
vie; elle y détruit et y consume insensiblement les passions et les vertus.

La Rochefoucauld

"An Empty Skull is the Devil's Workshop"

As of a man, so of a people. "The unredeemed ugliness is that of a slothful
people. Show me a people energetically busy—heaving, struggling, all
shoulders at the wheel; their heart pulsing, every muscle swelling with
man's energy and will—I will show you a people of whom great good is
already predicable; to whom all manner of good is certain if their energy
endure."

Carlyle

When the master puts a spade into his servant's hand,
He speaks his wish by the action, needing no words to declare it:
Thy hand, O man, like that spade, is God's signal to thee,
And thine own heart's thoughts are the interpretation thereof.

Mesnavi

The passage from Jelaluddin's *Mesnavi* does not bear the name of
the translator, but it was probably translated by FitzGerald himself
or by his friend, Edward Byles Cowell, whose influence was to play
a very important part in the direction of FitzGerald's literary genius.

II *The Bramford Years*

Cowell, an Orientalist, was a man of great intelligence and perse-
verance who had taught himself to read and write Persian while still
a schoolboy. Born and reared in a comfortable middle-class house-

hold with a background of refinement and culture, and himself an avid reader and brilliant student, Cowell had every reason to look forward to a university education and an eventual career in the academic profession. His interest in languages was prodigious, and his ability to acquire them seems to have been extraordinary. But Cowell's studies were cut short by the death of his father; at the age of sixteen, Cowell, who was the eldest son, had to assume responsibility for his father's business, which he ran for some years. Though his formal education had come to a temporary halt, Cowell continued to study on his own; and he learned several languages, including Spanish and Italian. He started taking lessons in Persian from a retired officer of the Indian army, Major Hockley, who later helped FitzGerald with his Persian studies. Cowell tried to learn Sanskrit also on his own, but was not successful; he had to wait until a later time to study the language which became his major interest.

At the time FitzGerald became acquainted with Cowell, he was a young man of twenty, and FitzGerald was seventeen years his senior. They probably met at the house of the Reverend John Charlesworth, rector of Flowton, near Ipswich. The Charlesworths were good friends of the FitzGerald family; and Elizabeth Charlesworth, the younger daughter of the rector, had visited the FitzGerald girls frequently at Woodbridge and Boulge. Elizabeth was endowed with charm and intelligence, and in 1845, when FitzGerald met Cowell, she was about thirty-two years of age. Though the name of FitzGerald's early and only love is not mentioned in any of his published correspondence, Cowell's biographer, George Cowell, thinks that Elizabeth was the young lady of FitzGerald's choice. He says that when Cowell announced that he was engaged to Elizabeth, FitzGerald remarked. "The deuce you are! Why! you have taken my Lady."[2] One cannot be certain whether this reaction was a spontaneous cry of anguish or polite gallantry on FitzGerald's part; but such gallantry would have been more in keeping with FitzGerald's character.

FitzGerald's first letter to Cowell in the published collection is dated 1846; and he mentions in it Cowell's translation of some of the odes of Hafez, the famous Persian poet of the fourteenth century. FitzGerald was greatly impressed with Cowell's knowledge and industry, and with his usual generosity of spirit, encouraged the young man in his efforts to establish a reputation in Oriental scholarship. Cowell and FitzGerald shared a common interest in Greek and

Latin, and their favorite pastime was to read the classics aloud and for Cowell to quote parallel passages from other authors. Later, they read Spanish and Persian together.

In 1847, after marrying Elizabeth Charlesworth, Cowell moved to Bramford; here the Cowells lived in a small cottage for more than three years. These were good years for the Cowells, but for FitzGerald, the Bramford years remained the happiest of his life, and he never ceased to remember them with great nostalgia. As Bramford was not far from FitzGerald's house, he could pay frequent visits to the Cowells and share in their favorite pastime of reading. One can picture them seated around the fire: Cowell is reading aloud; FitzGerald is wearing borrowed slippers; and Elizabeth perhaps wears a bright red dress, FitzGerald's favorite color, with a green ribbon cut into a leaf pattern, which, when the Cowells left Bramford, FitzGerald requested to have as a momento of the happy days. Cowell, on his part, seems to have had great respect for FitzGerald's abilities. In a letter to his mother dated April 23, 1850, he gives his impression of FitzGerald: "I should like you so to know him, he is a man of *real* power, one such as we seldom meet with in the world. There is something so very *solid* and *stately* about him, a kind of slumbering giant, or silent Vesuvius. It is only at times that the eruption comes, but when it does come, it overwhelms you!"[3]

During the years Cowell lived at Bramford, he continued his Oriental studies, published articles, and became known as a scholar. Although FitzGerald followed Cowell's progress with interest, offered him praise and encouragement, and, when necessary, criticism, he did not see himself as taking part in any of these activities. "Ten years ago I might have been vext to see you striding along in Sanscrit and Persian so fast; reading so much; remembering all; writing about it so well," FitzGerald wrote to Cowell in 1848 when a paper that Cowell had written on the *Mesnavi* was published. "But now I am glad to see any man do any thing well; and I know that it is my vocation to stand and wait, and know within myself whether it *is* done well."[4] FitzGerald was underestimating his own intellectual curiosity. By 1850, he was not only beginning to nibble at Spanish but, with Cowell's help, had also "bounced through" a play of Calderon.

FitzGerald's frequent visits to the "Scholar and his wife in their Village, in their delightful little house, in their pleasant fields by the

River side," as he once described the Cowells to his friends, were soon to end. Elizabeth had ambitious plans for Cowell's future, and she realized that, without a university degree, he would never gain the recognition that he sought. So it was decided, and the decision seems to have been for the most part hers, that Cowell should enter Oxford and earn a degree. Cowell hesitated about becoming an undergraduate at the age of twenty-five, and some of his friends also opposed the idea of his going to Oxford. FitzGerald and Donne suggested that Cowell might do better at one of the Scottish or London universities, but Elizabeth was entirely opposed to the idea. She had decided that Cowell should join Oxford, and it infuriated her that his friends, from whom she expected help, were proving a hindrance.

In her letter to a friend dated November 8, 1850, she vented her anger at FitzGerald and Donne: "But the mischief of it is that to prove their point they so *distort* College life, in the dreadfully long letters E. F. G. is rousing up his languid energies to send us, that Edward, who was just beginning, to my heartfelt thankfulness, to *rise* to the occasion, and really feel the fitness of his tastes and energies for the career before him, is now almost wholly turned back again, and ready to set off for Bury, as they want him to do, to talk with Mr. Donne,—and if he does that, I fear, but for God's help, the mischief will be *done!*—and that *I* should have done it! whose hope and dream has been his Oxford Career! . . ."[5] She concedes in a later letter that both Donne and FitzGerald "were acting according to their *own* view like true friends, and are both really men of the highest principle, as far as a *man* can be, who doubts if Scripture be altogether the highest guide," a remark which might have amused FitzGerald had he read it.

Elizabeth's fears about Edward FitzGerald's influence over Cowell proved wrong, for she finally overcame her husband's scruples and carried him off triumphantly to Oxford to get a degree in Oriental languages and history. Their departure from Bramford ended for FitzGerald three of the most delightful years of his life, years that he lived over and over again in his letters.

CHAPTER 3

Calderon and Jami

I Six Dramas of Calderon

ALTHOUGH the end of the Bramford years with the Cowells closed a pleasant chapter in FitzGerald's life, his interest in Spanish literature continued. FitzGerald had read Calderon with Cowell during his visits to Bramford, and he continued to translate Calderon at infrequent intervals. By the spring of 1853, he had decided to publish some five or six plays in a small volume, and he wrote to Elizabeth Cowell of his intention: ". . . I want Cowell for some passages: and my Translation would be so free as to be rather a dangerous Experiment. But I think you can hardly make Calderon interesting to English readers unless with a large latitude of interpretation."[1] By May, he had sent four plays to the printer and was putting the finishing touches to two more. Six Dramas of Calderon, Freely Translated by Edward FitzGerald, was published in July, 1853. Since the volume carried the name of the translator to distinguish it from another translation of the plays of Calderon by Denis F. M'Carthy, this publication was the only one to bear FitzGerald's name.

The six plays that FitzGerald selected for translation were The Painter of His Own Dishonour; Keep Your Own Secret; Gil Perez, the Gallician; Three Judgments at a Blow; The Mayor of Zalamea; and Beware of Smooth Water.[2] Fully aware that he would be attacked for taking liberties with Calderon, FitzGerald explained his method of selection and approach. His Advertisement to the plays began:

In apologizing for the publication of so free translations of so famous a poet as Calderon, I must plead, first, that I have not meddled with any of his more famous plays; not one of those on my list being mentioned with any praise, or included in any selection that I know of, except the homely Mayor

56

of Zalamea. . . . Secondly, I do not believe an exact translation of this poet can be very successful; retaining so much that, whether real or dramatic Spanish passion, is still bombast to English ears, and confounds otherwise distinct outlines of character; Conceits that were a fashion of the day; or idioms that, true and intelligible to one nation, check the current of sympathy in others to which they are unfamiliar; violations of probable, nay *possible*, that shock even healthy romantic license; repetitions of thoughts and images that Calderon used (and smiled at) as so much stage properties—so much, in short, that is not Calderon's better self, but concession to private haste or public taste. . . . Choosing therefore such less famous plays as still seemed to me suited to English taste, and to that form of verse in which our dramatic passion prefers to run, I have, while faithfully trying to retain what was fine and efficient, sunk, reduced, altered, and replaced much that seemed not; simplified some perplexities, and curtailed or omitted scenes that seemed to mar the breadth of general effect, supplying such omissions by some lines of after-narrative; and in some measure have tried to compensate for the fulness of sonorous Spanish, which Saxon English at least must forego, by a compression which has its charm to Saxon ears.

Admitting that "doubtless there are many inaccuracies I am not yet aware of," FitzGerald stated what was to be his consistent aim in all of his subsequent translations: "But if these plays prove interesting to the English reader, I and he may be very sure that, whatever of Spain and Calderon be lost, there must be a good deal retained; and I think he should excuse the licence of my version till some other interests him as well at less expense of fidelity." Plainly, the creation of a literary form and not a faithful transmission of the original was foremost in FitzGerald's mind. For his translation of the plays he chose blank verse and adopted many of the Shakespearean conventions. He may have considered it an interesting experiment to cast Calderon's plays in the mold of the English playwright to whom the Spanish playwright has so often been compared. With a fine regard for the dramatic, FitzGerald pared the dialogue of all unnecessary decorations; he used simple and dynamic language to propel the reader into the action of the play. He suited the style of the play to its content, so that *The Mayor of Zalamea*, which deals with the life of the plain folk, is entirely in prose.

FitzGerald's outstanding contribution to these plays is the beauty of his diction. The words ring clear and musical, and have a purity of sound worthy of FitzGerald's own admired masters of English style that he quoted in *Polonius*. The blank verse runs easily and smoothly, untrammeled by any of the hesitancies and obscurities that usually plague translations. In fact, FitzGerald resolutely turned away from the echoes of the Spanish to heed only the music of his native English, as is illustrated in this beautiful passage from *The Painter of His Own Dishonour* spoken by the prince. (act 1, scene 1):

>   I'll tell thee, Celio.
> He who far off beholds another dancing,
> Even one who dances best, and all the time
> Hears not the music that he dances to,
> Thinks him a madman, apprehending not
> The law that rules his else eccentric action.
> So he that's in himself insensible
> Of love's sweet influence, misjudges him
> Who moves according to love's melody:
> And knowing not that all these sighs and tears,
> Ejaculations, and impatiences,
> Are necessary changes of a measure,
> Which the divine musician plays, may call
> The lover crazy; which he would not do
> Did he within his own heart hear the tune
> Play'd by the great musician of the world.

FitzGerald's *Six Dramas of Calderon* exhibit, however, the weaknesses and strengths of all his translations. Being extremely free, they are termed "distortions" by readers who are familiar with the plays in the original language. But FitzGerald was not writing for those who could read Calderon in Spanish; instead, he wanted to convey to those who knew no Spanish the flavor of the original. He thought he could best do so by embodying in his English the virtues that were equivalent but not always identical to those of the original. As a result, he preserved the vitality and the action in his translations, as well as other qualities that are usually lost in transmission from one language to another. He contributed lyrical beauty in the form of songs and humor, a difficult feat to achieve in a translation.

The comic scenes alone make the reading of the plays worthwhile. The *graciosos* or clowns provide the comedy and, following the Shakespearean model, FitzGerald makes his buffoons speak in prose. Among the similarities between Calderon and Shakespeare that FitzGerald notes is the Falstaffian character of Lazaro in *Keep Your Own Secret* whose enemies multiply with each telling of his story. Lazaro occasionally indulges in verse, chiefly to puncture sentimentality:

Cesar: O Phoebus, swift across the skies
    Thy blazing carriage post away;
    Oh, drag with thee benighted day,
    And let the dawning night arise!
    Another sun shall mount the throne
      When thou art sunk beneath the sea;
    From whose effulgence, as thine own,
      The affrighted host of stars shall flee.

Lazaro: A pretty deal about your cares
      Does that same Phoebus care or know;
    He has to mind his own affairs,
      Whether you shake your head or no.
    You talk of hastening on the day?
      Why, heaven's coachman is the Sun,
    Who can't be put out of his way
      For you, sir, or for any one.

Act 1, Scene 3

Of the six plays, *The Mayor of Zalamea* seems to offer the best characterizations; and the use of prose may have given FitzGerald more latitude in delineating personality. The impoverished Don Mendo and his servant Nuño are another Don Quixote and Sancho Panza. But amusing as Nuño's expostulations are against hunger, the mayor, Pedro Crespo, leaves the most lasting impression on the reader. He displays the good yeoman virtues of independence and valor and the eccentricity of an English country squire. He makes no pretensions to nobility, and he refuses to buy a patent of gentility. He is not awed by title or position, however exalted. His tit-for-tat exchanges with Don Lope, the aristocratic commander of the regiment, provide some of the drollest and liveliest dialogue.

The mayor has his philosophical side, and his advice to his departing son Juan is reminiscent of Polonius. In a long prose passage, Pedro Crespo offers such platitudes as, "Be courteous in thy manner, and liberal of thy purse; for 'tis the hand to the bonnet and in the pocket that makes friends in this world; of which to gain one good, all the gold the sun breeds in India, or the universal sea sucks down, were a cheap purchase." FitzGerald's mayor, however, has

also a sense of humor; and he occasionally indulges in verse, as in
this exchange with his son:

Juan: I was looking for you, sir, but could not find you; where have you
          been?

Cres: To the barn, where high and dry,
          The jolly sheaves of corn do lie,
          Which the sun, arch-chemist old,
          Turn'd from black earth into gold,
          And the swinging flail one day
          On the barn-floor shall assay,
          Separating the pure ore
          From the drossy chaff away.
          This I've been about—And now,
          Juanito, what hast thou?

Juan: Alas, sir, I can't answer in so good rhyme or reason. I have been
          playing at fives, and lost every bout.

Cres: What signifies if you paid?

Juan: But I could not, and have come to you for the money.

Cres: Before I give it you, listen to me.
          There are things two
          Thou never must do;
          Swear to more than thou knowest.
          Play for more than thou owest;
          And never mind cost,
          So credit's not lost.

Juan: Good advice, sir, no doubt, that I shall lay by for its own sake as
          well as for yours, Meanwhile, I have also heard say,
          Preach not to a beggar till
          The beggar's empty hide you fill.

Cres: 'Fore Heaven, thou pay'st me in my own coin.

     The lyrics which provide melodious interludes in *The Mayor of
Zalamea* and the five other plays are Elizabethan in flavor. Since
music was FitzGerald's lifelong interest, he displays in the "Songs"
both his knowledge of music and the mastery of the lyrical form. The

following "Song" from *The Mayor of Zalamea* should sound familiar to those acquainted with the *Rubáiyát:*

> Ah for the red spring rose,
>   Down in the garden growing,
> Fading as fast as it blows,
>   Who shall arrest its going?
> Peep from thy window and tell,
>   Fairest of flowers, Isabel.

Sometimes the words simply express the emotions of the singers:

> Titiri tiri, marching is weary,
>   Weary, weary, and long is the way:
> Titiri tiri, hither, my deary,
>   What meat have you got for the soldier to-day?
> "Meat have I none, my merry men,"
> Titiri tiri, then kill the old hen.
> "Alas and a day! the old hen is dead!"
> Then give us a cake from the oven instead.
>   Titiri titiri titiri tiri,
> Give us a cake from the oven instead.

FitzGerald sent copies of his translation to his friends, and they liked it. George Borrow, the author of *The Romany Rye*, praised the book, which greatly pleased FitzGerald. "I am really obliged to you for your letter," FitzGerald wrote to him on August 3, 1853, "the more so as I think I have heard you do not much like writing. Though I of course thought the Translations well done (or I should not have printed them), I naturally desired the approval of a competent Judge; since the best of us may make sad mistakes in the estimation of our own handiwork; and it is not pleasant to dub oneself an Ass in print." To George Crabbe, the poet's son and FitzGerald's close friend, who was also the recipient of a copy of the translation, FitzGerald wrote on July 22 of the same year: ". . . I am very glad you like the plays and am encouraged to hope that other persons who are not biassed by pedantic prejudices or spites might like them too. But I fully expect that (as I told you, I think) the London press, etc., will either sink them, or condemn them as on too free a principle: and all the more if they have not read the originals. For these are safe courses to adopt."

FitzGerald's prediction turned out to be true. The *Athenaeum* reviewed the plays in a short paragraph. Seizing upon FitzGerald's apology, the reviewer dismissed the translation with the curt remark that he had not taken the trouble to compare the translation with the original, "holding it quite unnecessary to treat as a serious work a book whose author confesses that he has 'sunk, reduced and replaced much that seemed not fine or efficient. . . .' "[3] FitzGerald, who was not surprised at what he termed "the Athenaeum's determined spit at me," concluded philosophically that "one must take these chances if one will play at so doubtful a game"; but he was consoled when another translator of Calderon, Richard Chenevix Trench, praised FitzGerald in his book, *Calderon: His Life and Genius*. To Trench, the *Six Dramas* was "far the most important and worthiest contribution to the knowledge of the Spanish poet . . . yet received."[4] Though Trench did not agree with FitzGerald's use of blank verse for his plays, he nevertheless thought that FitzGerald's language was "English of an exquisite purity and vigor" and that it dealt "with poetry in a poet's spirit."

II   *Persian and* Salámán and Absál

When the Cowells were at Oxford, FitzGerald corresponded with them and visited them occasionally. W. R. Morfill, who was an undergraduate at the university, recalled seeing FitzGerald on one of his visits "wrapped in a plaid and a mysterious atmosphere of cynicism . . . all who knew him believed him capable of great things. . . . "[5] Cowell urged FitzGerald to learn Persian, but FitzGerald's interest in the language remained that of a detached observer. When Cowell's selections from Hafez were published, FitzGerald wrote to him in 1852 approving of his translation and encouraging him to work on the *Mesnavi:* "I am almost ashamed to go and see you, for I never read anything but nonsense. I shall always be glad to listen: but I believe I shall never more be able to contribute to any better subject."

Not long after this letter of 1852, FitzGerald allowed himself to be persuaded to learn Persian. As Cowell recalled later, it was on a rainy Sunday that he suggested Persian to FitzGerald and guaranteed to teach him the grammar in a day. The book he selected was Sir William Jones's *Persian Grammar*, in which the illustrations are from Hafez. FitzGerald, who became interested, then studied Hafez more closely. FitzGerald mentions his Persian studies for the first time in a letter to Cowell dated December 29, 1852, written after a visit to the Tennysons, who had a new baby: "I told A. T. he was to learn Persian at Oxford and follow the example of yours truly." The letter is signed in Persian characters.

The following year, FitzGerald studied Persian grammar, did a little translation every day, and sent his exercises to Cowell for correction. He also took lessons from Major Hockley, who lived in Ipswich. After the printing of the *Six Dramas of Calderon,* FitzGerald was able to give his full attention to Persian. Continuing to use Sir William Jones's *Persian Grammar* as his main guide, he read selections from the Persian classics. The illustrations in the grammar aroused his interest in Saadi; he acquired a copy of E. B. Eastwick's 1854 translation of the *Gulistan;* but he found Eastwick's style not to his liking. He also bought from the bookseller Bernard Quaritch the *Shah Nameh* of Firdusui, whom he greatly admired.

FitzGerald must have started reading Jami's *Salámán and Absál* in the spring of 1854, for he mentions the poem in his letters to Cowell. FitzGerald apparently used Forbes Falconer's edition, which was published in London in 1850. Jami's mysticism interested him, but he found it unfathomable at times, as apparently did his teacher, Major Hockley. FitzGerald was soon laying Jami aside to look into Hafez. While staying with Tennyson at Freshwater, he translated some Hafez with Tennyson, who particularly liked this Persian poet, and sent the translations to Cowell for correction. But Hafez did not hold FitzGerald's attention for long; he returned to Jami, "whose ingenuous prattle," he wrote to Cowell in 1855, "I am stilting into too Miltonic verse." He had hoped that Cowell would collaborate with him in translating *Salámán and Absál,* but Cowell was not interested. FitzGerald started working on his own; and, by the spring of 1855, he had completed his version of the poem. He offered *Salámán and Absál* to *Fraser's Magazine,* which rejected it. FitzGerald kept the poem for a few months, recast some of the stories which Cowell thought too heavy, and sent *Salámán* to the printer in January, 1856. During the next four months, FitzGerald corrected and revised the translation. He sent the proofsheets to Cowell for approval, enclosing as well lists of questions dealing with the translation and the printing. FitzGerald strove to keep as close as possible to the original, but he sometimes found himself confused about the deeper meanings of the Persian. He retained the Persian names, using "Shah" for king, "Yusuf and Suleyman" for Joseph and

Solomon; for, as he stated, "it is well to rub off as little Oriental Colour as possible."

Salámán and Absál was finally ready on April 4, 1856. The small volume was bound in royal blue cloth with the title tooled in fanciful gold letters on the spine and the front cover. The name of the translator was not mentioned, but the preface was cast in the form of a letter to Cowell: "What scholarship it has is yours, my Master in Persian, and so much beside; who are no further answerable for *all* than by well liking and wishing publisht what you may scarce have Leisure to find fault with." The preface evinced more personal emotion than is usual in prefaces; FitzGerald had learned that Cowell, who had graduated from Oxford, had been appointed professor of English history at Presidency College, Calcutta, and would be leaving for India with his wife. FitzGerald's preface reflected his sadness at parting with his two good friends: "Ah, happy Days! When shall we Three meet again—when dip in that unreturning Tide of Time and Circumstance!—In those Meadows far from the World, it seemed, as Salámán's Island—before an Iron Railway broke the Heart of that Happy Valley whose Gossip was the Millwheel, and Visitors the Summer Airs that momentarily ruffled the sleepy Stream that turned it as they chased one another over to lose themselves in Whispers in the Copse beyond."

FitzGerald had modest words about his own effort:

But to turn from you Two to a Public—nearly as numerous—(with whom, by the way, this Letter may die without a name that *you* know very well how to supply),—here is the best I could make of Jámi's Poem—"Ouvrage de peu d'étendue," says the Biographie Universelle, and, whatever that means, here collapsed into a nutshell Epic indeed; whose Story however, if nothing else, may interest some Scholars as one of Persian Mysticism— perhaps the grand Mystery of all Religions—an Allegory fairly devised and carried out—dramatically culminating as it goes on; and told as to this day the East loves to tell her Story, illustrated by Fables and Tales, so often (as we read in the latest Travels) at the expense of the poor Arab of the Desert.

The story is a simple one, though it is interlaced with anecdotes which the poet uses to emphasize a moral or a particular point. The king of Yunan, or Greece which is a favorite land of Persian folktales, has grown prosperous under the wise guidance of a sage; but the king is saddened by the lack of a son. The sage warns him against indulgence in the lust of the flesh without which there could be no offspring. Equating lust with marriage, the sage elaborates against the wiles and strategems of women with a misogynistic fervor which makes one wonder whether it is mysticism on Jami's part or the outcry of a nagged husband. To console the king, the sage, through his supernatural powers, creates for him a son who is not born of woman and who is free from the blemishes common to mankind. Because of his perfection, the boy is given the name of Salaman, derived from the words "Salamat" ("wholesome") and "Asman" ("the heavens"). Since the child has no mother, a young and beautiful woman, Absal, is chosen as his nurse. She lavishes the utmost love and care on her ward, and the young man grows up perfect in all the accomplishments required of a young prince.

When Salaman is fourteen years old and is considered to have reached puberty, his nurse Absal, now a mature young woman of great beauty, falls in love with him. By her womanly wiles, she succeeds in winning the heart of the young prince. He immerses himself in her love, and consequently neglects his princely duties. Inevitably, the king and the sage learn of the affair, and they endeavor to dissuade him by advice and admonition. Salaman tries hard to forget his love; but, finding himself unable to do so, he decides to flee with Absal to a deserted island. Here the two lovers live an idyllic life. But the king, who has been searching for them, discovers their hiding place with the aid of his magic mirror; he casts a spell upon Salaman, and renders him incapable of approaching his beloved. Salaman is contrite over his transgressions; and his heart turns towards the king whose mercy and forgiveness he seeks.

But Salaman cannot overcome his love for Absal, and decides in desperation to commit suicide. He and Absal build a bonfire and enter into the flames hand in hand. The king, who has been aware of Salaman's plight, allows the flames to devour Absal but saves Salaman. The prince, now separated forever from his beloved, is seized with such inconsolable grief that the king cannot bear to see his agony and seeks help from the sage. The wise man takes Salaman under his tutelage; to assuage the young man's sorrow, the sage conjures up Absal's image; but, at the same time, expounds the celestial beauties of Zohra or Venus, which symbolizes Divine Perfection. Gradually, the longing for Absal is purged from Salaman's soul; and heavenly love takes the place of his earthly one. Cleansed at last of all earthly ties, Salaman is deemed fit by the king to take his rightful place on the throne.

At the conclusion of the poem, Jami elucidates his allegory by
pointing out that Salaman is the soul, that Absal represents the body
with its taste for sensual pleasure, and that their close affair continues unchecked until the body tires of sensual pleasure. Not until
all earthly ties are burned away in the fire of strict discipline does
the soul finally turn to the eternal truth and reach unity with the
spirit of immortal beauty.

Jami's philosophy is undoubtedly Sufistic or mystical, but it would
be an injustice to Jami the poet to look solely for mysticism in his
poem, and to disregard the literary merits. The purity of Jami's
language, the telling points brought out neatly in the anecdotes,
the humor, and the psychological truths embodied in the episodes
touch responsive chords in the reader. Even the most uninitiated
can understand and enjoy the poem because of the genius of the
poet who allows each man to take from the poem according to his
own ability. To use an analogy which Jami the mystic might have
favored himself, the meaning is like a bountiful spring: each man
carries away as much of it as his capacity allows.

To the modern reader who would not wish to delve into Sufistic
mysteries, the poem would perhaps appeal most when regarded as
the recollections of an old philosopher who found a positive aspect
to old age—the enjoyment of the joys of the intellect when the
pleasures of the senses are no longer possible. Jami was in his sixties
when he wrote the poem, and an old man by the standards of the
time. He complains in the poem of the infirmities attendant upon
old age—failing eyesight, falling teeth, painful joints. Thus, when
he writes of Salaman's despair at finding himself near his beloved
but powerless to approach her, the reader does not have to know the
philosophy of mysticism to appreciate the poet's meaning. The dia-
tribes against lust and women assume an additional meaning because of the earlier passage in the Persian version which alludes to
the renouncing of wine and pleasure by the young king, Yacub Bey,
to whom the entire poem is dedicated. The figure of the sage is
Jami's compliment to the young king's vizier. The poem is thus
firmly anchored to earth, lofty though its flights are to those who
wish to explore the higher mysteries with Jami.

The many layers of meaning are the poem's strength, but they are
also the translator's despair. Considering the difficulties he had to
overcome, not the least of which was his own inadequate knowledge
of Persian, FitzGerald succeeds surprisingly well in conveying the

meaning of the poem. FitzGerald shortened his version considerably, and left out the invocations at the beginning of the poem to the Prophet Mohammed and his successors, and to the young king Yacub Bey of the "White Sheep" Turcomans. FitzGerald did include, however, the account of the poet's dream of the king's father, Uzun Hasan, who had extended his hospitality to Jami some years previously, and to whom Jami pays tribute. The whole poem is meant to be a coronation present to the young king, who ascended the throne after his father's death. FitzGerald retained, as well, Jami's lament over his failing powers. He started the poem with its beginning invocation to God and the illustrative story of the bewildered Kurd; but he discarded several of the stories and large portions of the poem, and translated or adapted only those parts that he thought suitable for the English reader.

In the invocatory passage to God, Jami expounds the philosophy of the undivided love of the mystic for the Deity. Earthly love is only the prelude to Divine love; God is the ultimate Beloved that the mystic seeks, and the perfect consummation occurs when the mystic merges into the Beloved. FitzGerald stays close to the original in this passage. The illustrative story of the Kurd, lost in the city, expresses the spiritual dilemma of the mystic who has not yet achieved union with the Beloved. FitzGerald introduced an innovation here; he changed the tempo of the apologues, so that their brisk and lively pace breaks the solemn measure of the main poem and prevents monotony. The illustrative stories, which are in the same meter as the rest of the poem in the original, become musical interludes in FitzGerald's version.

FitzGerald's *Salámán and Absál* begins thus:

> Oh Thou whose Memory quickens Lovers' Souls,
> Whose Fount of Joy renews the Lover's Tongue,
> Thy shadow falls across the World, and They
> Bow down to it; and of the Rich in Beauty
> Thou art the Riches that make Lovers mad.
> Not till thy Secret Beauty through the Cheek
> Of LAILA smite does she inflame MAJNÚN,
> And not till Thou have sugar'd SHÍRÍN's Lip
> The Hearts of those Two Lovers fill with Blood.
> For Lov'd and Lover are not but by Thee,
> Nor Beauty;—Mortal Beauty but the Veil
> Thy Heavenly hides behind, and from itself

Feeds, and our Hearts yearn after as a Bride
That glances past us Veil'd—but ever so
As none the Beauty from the Veil may know.
How long wilt thou continue thus the World
To cozen with the Fantom of a Veil
From which Thou only Peepest?—Time it is
To unfold thy perfect Beauty. I would be
Thy Lover and Thine only—I, mine Eyes
Seal'd in the Light of Thee to all but Thee,
Yea, in the Revelation of Thyself
Self-Lost, and Conscience-quit of Good and Evil.
Thou movest under all the Forms of Truth,
Under the Forms of all Created Things;
Look whence I will, still nothing I discern
But Thee in all the Universe, in which
Thyself Thou dost invest, and through the Eyes
Of MAN, the subtle Censor scrutinize.
To thy Harím DIVIDUALITY
No entrance finds—no Word of THIS and THAT;
Do Thou my separate and Derivéd Self
Make One with thy Essential! Leave me room
On that Diván, which leaves no Room for Two;
Lest, like the Simple Kurd of whom they tell,
I grow perplext, oh God! 'twixt "I" and "THOU:"
If I—this Dignity and Wisdom whence?
If THOU—then what this abject Impotence?

A Kurd perplext by Fortune's Frolics
Left his Desert for the City.
Sees a City full of Noise and
Clamour, agitated People,
Hither, Thither, Back and Forward
Running, some intent on Travel,
Others home again returning,
Right to Left, and Left to Right,
Life-disquiet everywhere!
Kurd, when he beholds the Turmoil,
Creeps aside, and, Travel-weary,
Fain would go to Sleep; "But," saith he,
"How shall I in all this Hubbub
"Know myself again on waking?"
So by way of Recognition
Ties a Pumpkin round his Foot,
And turns to Sleep. A Knave that heard him

> *Crept behind, and slily watching*
> *Slips the Pumpkin off the Sleeper's*
> *Ancle, ties it round his own,*
> *And so down to sleep beside him.*
> *By and by the Kurd awaking*
> *Looks directly for his Signal—*
> *Sees it on another's Ancle—*
> *Cries aloud, "Oh Good-for-Nothing*
> *"Rascal to perplex me so!*
> *"That by you I am bewilder'd,*
> *"Whether I be I or no!*
> *If I—the Pumpkin why on YOU?*
> *If YOU—then where am I, and WHO?"*

In his revised version of *Salámán and Absál*, which FitzGerald first had printed in 1871 on a small scale, and which he included with the fourth edition of the *Rubáiyát* in 1879, the verse becomes more polished and musical; but it also diverges more from the original. For example, "Kurd" becomes "Arab," and "City," "Baghdad":

> From the solitary Desert
> Up to Baghdád came a simple
> Arab; there amid the rout
> Grew bewilder'd of the countless
> People, hither, thither, running,
> Coming, going, meeting, parting,
> Clamour, clatter, and confusion,
> All about him and about. . . .

Though *Salámán* is a mystical allegory, it is not a dry and dull enumeration of the path of asceticism. The story is about a love affair, and the poem has several erotic passages. These are allegorical, but the human details give life to the poem for the general reader, and FitzGerald was undoubtedly aware of the fact. By his minute descriptions of such purely earthly matters as Absal's beauty and her machinations to attract Salaman's attention, Jami shows that he is a man as well as a mystic. FitzGerald omitted none of these passages, and they are more appealing than his mystical expositions. In this description of Absal's efforts to attract Salaman, the quaint metaphors deliberately used to allude to her physical charms provide an undertone of amusement:

Now was SALÁMÁN in his Prime of Growth,
His Cypress Stature risen to high Top,
And the new-blooming Garden of his Beauty
Began to bear; and Absál long'd to gather;
But the Fruit grew upon too high a Bough,
To which the Noose of her Desire was short.
She too rejoiced in Beauty of her own
No whit behind SALÁMÁN, whom she now
Began enticing with her Sorcery.
Now from her Hair would twine a musky Chain,
To bind his Heart—now twist it into Curls
Nestling innumerable Temptations;
Doubled the Darkness of her Eyes with Surma
To make him lose his way, and over them
Adorn'd the Bows that were to shoot him then;
Now to the Rose-leaf of her Cheek would add
Fresh Rose, and then a Grain of Musk lay there,
The Bird of the Belovéd Heart to snare.
Now with a Laugh would break the Ruby Seal
That lockt up Pearl; or busied in the Room
Would smite her Hand perhaps—on that pretence
To lift and show the Silver in her Sleeve;
Or hastily rising clash her Golden Anclets
To draw the Crownéd Head under her Feet.
Thus by innumerable Bridal wiles
She went about soliciting his Eyes,
Which she would scarce let lose her for a Moment;
For well she knew that mainly by THE EYE
Love makes his Sign, and by no other Road
Enters and takes possession of the Heart.

The elegant passage that describes the first secret meeting between
the lovers ends with lines that are reminiscent of the *Rubáiyát*:

Now when SALÁMÁN's Heart turn'd to ABSÁL,
Her Star was happy in the Heavens—Old Love
Put forth afresh—Desire doubled his Bond:
And of the running Time she watch'd an Hour
To creep into the Mansion of her Moon
And satiate her soul upon his Lips.
And the Hour came; she stole into his Chamber—
Ran up to him, Life's offer in her Hand—
And, falling like a Shadow at his Feet,
She laid her Face beneath, SALÁMÁN then
With all the Courtesies of Princely Grace

Put forth his Hand—he rais'd her in his Arms—
He held her trembling there—and from that Fount
Drew first Desire; then Deeper from her Lips,
That, yielding, mutually drew from his
A wine that ever drawn from never fail'd—

So through the Day—so through another still—
The day Became a Seventh—the Seventh a Moon—
The Moon a Year—while they rejoiced together,
Thinking their Pleasure never was to end.
But rolling Heaven whisper'd from his Ambush,
"So in my License is it not set down.
"Ah for the sweet Societies I make
"At morning and before the Nightfall break;
"Ah for the Bliss that with the Setting Sun
"I mix, and, with his Rising, all is done!"

After Salaman's ordeal by fire, the sage, symbolic of reason, comes
to his rescue. With reason and spirituality in the ascendant, Salaman
the soul, achieves oneness with the Supreme Being. A golden light,
indicative of serenity, envelops Salaman as he ascends the throne:

Then THE SHAH crown'd him with the Golden Crown,
And set the Golden Throne beneath his Feet,
And over all the Heads of the Assembly,
And in the Ears of all of them, his Jewels
With the Diamond of Wisdom cut, and said. . . .

Here follows a lecture on morality which Jami intended as advice for
the young king starting his reign. There follows an epilogue, in
which the inner meaning of the poem is explained. The poem ends
on the note of eternal beauty:

For what is ZUHRAH?—the Divine Perfection,
Wherewith the Soul inspir'd and all array'd
In Intellectual Light is Royal blest,
And mounts THE THRONE, and wears THE CROWN, and Reigns
Lord of the Empire of Humanity.
This is the Meaning of This Mystery,
Which to know wholly ponder in thy Heart,
Till all its ancient Secret be enlarged.
Enough—The written Summary I close,
And set my Seal:
                    THE TRUTH GOD ONLY KNOWS.

In a later version, FitzGerald decided to heighten the light which surrounds Zuhrah in his concluding lines, and rewrote the passage:

> For what is ZUHRAH?—What but that Divine
> Original, of which the Soul of Man
> Darkly possesst, by that fierce Discipline
> At last he disengages from the Dust,
> And flinging off the baser rags of Sense,
> And all in Intellectual Light array'd,
> As Conqueror and King he mounts the Throne,
> And wears the Crown of Human Glory—Whence,
> Throne over Throne surmounting, he shall reign
> One with the LAST and FIRST INTELLIGENCE.

Placed beside the "night" quatrains of the *Rubáiyát*, in the fourth edition of which *Salámán and Absál* was also included, the bright and optimistic ending of *Salámán* achieves an artistic contrast.

FitzGerald had predicted about his *Salámán and Absál* that half a dozen would buy the book and that the critics in the papers would sneer. The review that appeared in the *Athenaeum* of August 2, 1856, was not favorable. The reviewer devoted the greater part of his article to recounting the story of *Salámán and Absál*, and to pointing out its allegorical nature. He turned his attention to FitzGerald's version only in the last paragraph: "It remains to say a word of the present translation, or rather epitome, for whole pages are omitted. It shows some poetic feeling, a diligent use of the dictionary, but a very moderate acquaintance with Persian. The few difficult lines that occur in the poem are passed over without notice, and mistakes are rather numerous." The reviewer pointed out spellings which he thought unorthodox, and misinterpretations of meaning. He declared that "The translator's efforts in the 'Hiawatha' metre are not successful," and he ended his review with the condescending line: "As a first attempt, however, to make Jámi accessible to the English reader, this little volume is deserving of commendation."[16] The review made little impression upon FitzGerald, for matters of a more important nature claimed his attention. Cowell would leave that summer for India, and FitzGerald himself would become involved in some very important events, both personal and literary.

CHAPTER 4

The Rubáiyát of Omar Khayyám

I *FitzGerald's Marriage*

THE most important literary event of 1856 for FitzGerald was his introduction to Omar Khayyam. While working in the Bodleian library, Cowell had found a copy of the quatrains of the eleventh-century Persian poet, Khayyam. The manuscript was a fourteenth-century one, and it belonged to the Ouseley collection. Cowell, who had never seen a manuscript of Khayyam's quatrains, was pleased with his find, and made a copy of it for his own use. He showed the quatrains to FitzGerald, and that summer, when FitzGerald visited the Cowells at Rushmere, they read Omar Khayyam together and discussed his philosophy. Omar undoubtedly made an impression on FitzGerald, who must have found his humor and his ironic jests at man's helplessness quite different from the solemn tones of *Salámán and Absál*. He wrote to Alfred Tennyson about his Persian studies on July 26, 1856: "I have been the last Fortnight with the Cowells. We read some curious Infidel and Epicurean Tetrastichs by a Persian of the Eleventh Century—as Savage against Destiny &c as Manfred—but mostly of Epicurean Pathos of this kind—'Drink—for the Moon will often come round to look for us in this Garden and find us not.' "

That summer's visit with the Cowells was FitzGerald's last for a long time. The Cowells left for India in August, and as a parting gift, Cowell gave FitzGerald a transcript of Omar Khayyam's quatrains similar to the one that he had made for himself. In Calcutta, Cowell remembered to look in the library of the Royal Asiatic Society for copies of Omar Khayyam's poetry; and he found one—a "dingy little manuscript," with the last page or two missing—that contained several hundred more tetrastichs than the Ouseley manuscript. In Cowell's letter to FitzGerald announcing his discovery, he wrote a

Persian passage from the Calcutta manuscript that related a story about Omar Khayyam on the authority of Nizami of Samarkand. Cowell included a translation of this passage in his article on Omar Khayyam published in the *Calcutta Review* of 1858. Later, in his introduction to the *Rubáiyát of Omar Khayyám*, FitzGerald quoted Cowell's translation of the account.

In the meantime, FitzGerald was occupied with matters of a personal nature. On November 4, 1856, after a long engagement lasting seven years, FitzGerald married Lucy Barton, the daughter of his Quaker friend, Bernard Barton. The marriage held little promise of success. FitzGerald's close friends, who knew his idiosyncrasies as well as his sterling qualities, realized that he was making a mistake; and the more outspoken ones tried to dissuade him. Although FitzGerald himself had misgivings about his marriage, his sense of honor would not let him withdraw from the contract unless Lucy signified her willingness to break the engagement. But to a woman as strong minded as Lucy, FitzGerald's hesitation seemed like the behavior of a man inclined to look on the worst side of things; as for herself, she had no fears for the future.

How the engagement between two such strongly contrasting personalities had come about no one knows for certain, but close friends and relatives of both FitzGerald and Lucy shared the view that FitzGerald had become unwittingly involved in the contract and found it impossible to withdraw honorably. Perhaps his promise to Bernard Barton to watch over Lucy's interests and protect her from harm had occasioned his proposal. FitzGerald's grandniece, Mary Eleanor FitzGerald Kerrich, suggests that Bernard Barton had placed Lucy's hand in FitzGerald's as they both stood at the poet's bedside in his last moments, and FitzGerald had acquiesced helplessly in this implied promise of marriage which a more worldly man would have immediately disclaimed.[1]

Undoubtedly, the future welfare of the daughter of a very dear friend must have been an important consideration to FitzGerald, since Barton had suffered financial loss in the last year of his life and had left his daughter virtually penniless.

After Barton's death, FitzGerald had assisted Lucy in editing the letters and poems of her father and had published them with a memoir about Bernard Barton, thus perpetuating the memory of the Quaker poet, as well as helping Lucy financially. F. R. Barton, in his edition of FitzGerald's letters to Bernard Barton, holds the view that FitzGerald proposed to Lucy during the time they were preparing the edition of her father's poems. "Nothing definite is known as to what impelled FitzGerald to take this step," he writes. "They had both passed their fortieth year: she a few months the senior. In point of intellect, culture, benevolence, and address, Lucy Barton was doubtless attractive, but she lacked physical charms. Her features were heavy, she was tall and big of bone, and her voice was loud and deep. The key of the puzzle is probably to be found in FitzGerald's quixotic temperament."[2]

Reading between the lines of the fragmentary records available, F. R. Barton reconstructs a series of events leading to the marriage. Starting with Barton's uneasiness about the future of his daughter and FitzGerald's assurance to him to help her, F. R. Barton concludes that after Barton's death, FitzGerald had made an impetuous offer to make up the deficiency in her income from his own; but her sense of propriety forbade her to accept such an offer. "One can imagine the effect of her refusal upon a temperament so sensitive as FitzGerald's," F. R. Barton writes. "He accused himself of having committed an indelicacy—a breach of good taste. His disordered fancy prompted him to believe that he had grossly outraged the feelings of his old companion's daughter by offering her money. The thought was intolerable to him. He must make amends at any cost. And so, heedless of the consequences, he proposed marriage, and she—blind to the distraction of mind that had impelled him—accepted his offer."[3] Whatever the circumstances surrounding the engagement, FitzGerald was obviously acting from a purely altruistic motive, for there had never been any romantic attachment between the two. In none of his published letters pertaining to this period is there a hint of any romantic feeling toward Lucy.

If FitzGerald did propose to Lucy Barton after her father's death, he was not able to carry out his promise of marriage for several years. His father's bankruptcy, occasioned by unwise commercial ventures, had also reduced FitzGerald's income by a considerable amount. Not until the death of his mother in 1855 was FitzGerald able to establish a home. As for Lucy Barton, following the death of her father, she had become companion to the two grandnieces of a wealthy Quaker, Hudson Gurney, and had lived at Keswick Hall in Norwich very much like one of the family. Her exposure to high society had apparently changed her considerably by giving her a taste for fine living; she looked forward to the time when, as the wife of a gentleman of means, she would be able to take part in the round of parties and dances that were the chief amusement of the local gentry.

FitzGerald, too, had changed in the seven years. Always of a retiring nature, he had become more of a recluse; he spent his time reading or taking walks, and visited only a few close friends. He had no use for the fashionable gentry and their conventions, and he cared little for what they said about him. His attire varied little from day to day; he always wore an old black coat with a crumpled collar and a tall slouch hat which he secured around his head with a handkerchief on windy days. In winter, an old shawl was his constant companion. Abstemious in habit, he lived very simply; he ate sparingly, mostly bread and fruit; but he never imposed his own way of life on others. His table was loaded with meat and game when guests were present, and he often sent presents of the local delicacies to his friends. In the mode of life that he had adopted, he had freed himself from convention; and he had no wish to impose restrictions on others.

In contemplating marriage with Lucy, FitzGerald was undoubtedly aware of the differences in their habits and attitudes. But he apparently hoped that, as he was fulfilling an obligation of friendship by giving her security and status, she, on her part, would respect his way of life and leave him alone. He had known her when she had lived a simple life with her father, and he evidently thought that it would not be difficult for her to adjust to a quiet, uneventful life with him. If FitzGerald had expected such an accommodation on Lucy's part, he was soon to be disappointed. She had her own ideas about how a gentleman should live, and she tried to make FitzGerald conform to them, which he would not do. Both were strong minded, neither would yield, and FitzGerald was very unhappy. They separated for a time, then tried to live together again; but their differences were irreconcilable. After less than a year of marriage, the two parted. Though they were never divorced, they did not live together again. FitzGerald blamed himself for all that had gone wrong; he made a handsome settlement on Lucy and returned to his old ways. Lucy FitzGerald lived until 1898, dying at the age of ninety.

The months of married life were perhaps among the unhappiest of FitzGerald's life. The two friends who had been closest to him and might have provided solace were thousands of miles away in India.

His letters to the Cowells during this period show how sorely he missed them and how miserable he was. "I believe there are new Channels fretted in my Cheeks with many unmanly Tears since then," he wrote to Cowell on January 22, 1857, " 'remembering the Days that are no more,' in which you two are so mixt up." For comfort, FitzGerald turned to Persian, which he associated with his friends and with the happy times he had spent in their company.

He started reading *Mantic uttair* of the Persian mystic Farid uddin Attar with the help of an analysis of the poem published by the French Orientalist Garcin de Tassy. Learning that de Tassy was printing a Persian text of the *Mantic*, FitzGerald wrote to him to ask where he could obtain a copy; at the same time, he sent de Tassy a copy of his *Salámán and Absál*. In his reply, de Tassy mentioned his intention of translating the *Mantic* into prose; his French translation was published in 1863. Though FitzGerald used de Tassy's Persian text of *Mantic*, he did not consult de Tassy's translation for his own version which is in verse, and which he had completed before the publication of the French translation.

By the end of March, 1857, FitzGerald had finished a rough draft of *Mantic uttair*, which he called *Bird-Parliament*. He put it away, hoping to come on it one day with fresh eyes, as he said, and to trim it with some natural impulse.

II *Translation of the* Rubáiyát

FitzGerald next turned his attention to the *Rubáiyát* of Omar Khayyam. He was working with Cowell's transcript of the quatrains; and, wishing to find out if there were any other manuscripts extant, he wrote a letter to Garcin de Tassy. Since De Tassy had not heard of Omar Khayyam, FitzGerald copied the quatrains and sent them to him. De Tassy was so taken with the stanzas that he wrote a paper, "Note sur les rubâ'iyât de 'Omar Khaïyâm," which he read before the Persian ambassador at a meeting of the Oriental Society. When the article was published in the *Journal Asiatique* of 1857, he wished to acknowledge his debt to FitzGerald and Cowell in his article; but he was urged by FitzGerald not to do so. As FitzGerald later explained to Elizabeth Cowell, "he did not wish E. B. C. to be made answerable for errors which E. F. G. (the *'copist'*) may have made: and that E. F. G. neither merits nor desires any honourable mention as a Persian Scholar: being none."[4]

FitzGerald continued his Persian studies with Cowell by mail. His letters to the Cowells in the spring and summer of 1857 resemble his diarylike letters to Thackeray during the Larksbeare period. FitzGerald added to his missives from day to day, keeping them for as long as two months; he described his progress in reading the *Rubáiyát*, wrote down his comments, and sought clarification of words and lines he could not understand. In his note of June 5 to a very lengthy letter which he had started on May 7, 1857, laid aside, and resumed a month later during a visit to his friend W. K. Browne, FitzGerald mentions working on a Latin translation of Omar:

When in Bedfordshire I put away almost all Books except—Omar Khayyám!—which I could not help looking over in a Paddock covered with Buttercups & brushed by a delicious Breeze, while a dainty racing Filly of W. Browne's came startling up to wonder and snuff about me. "Tempus est quo Orientis Aurâ mundus renovatur, Quo de fonte pluviali dulcis Imber reseratur; *Musi-manus* undecumque ramos insuper splendescit; Jesuspiritusque Salustaris terram pervagatur." Which is to be read as Monkish Latin, like "Dies Irae," etc., retaining the Italian Value of the Vowels, not the Classical. You will think me a perfectly Aristophanic Old Man when I tell you how many of Omar I could not help running into such bad Latin. I should not confide such follies to you who won't think them so, and who will be pleased at least with my still harping on our old Studies. You would be sorry, too, to think that Omar breathes a sort of Consolation to me! Poor Fellow; I think of him, and Oliver Basselin, and Anacreon; lighter Shadows among the Shades, perhaps, over which Lucretius presides so grimly.

The transcript of the Calcutta manuscript of the *Rubáiyát* that Cowell had sent from India reached FitzGerald in June, 1857. The copy was in such inferior script that it was indecipherable in places, and it must have taxed FitzGerald's eyes and his knowledge of Persian to read it. But he studied it, collated it with the Ouseley manuscript, and made annotations as he progressed. He noted the differences in the two manuscripts in his long letter to Cowell, suggesting what might be the correct reading of a word or line, and received Cowell's reply by mail. By July 13, 1857, he had accomplished enough to write to Cowell, "By tomorrow I shall have finisht my first Physiognomy of Omar, whom I decidedly prefer to any Persian I have yet seen, unless perhaps Salámán. . . ."[5] As he read the transcript of the Calcutta manuscript and compared it with that of Ouseley's, he

was constantly thinking of the Rushmere days: "Here is the An-
niversary of our Adieu at Rushmere," he added to the July 13 letter
on July 14. "And I have been (rather hastily) getting to an end of my
first survey of the Calcutta Omar, by way of counterpart to our joint
survey of the Ouseley MS. then. I suppose we spoke of it this day
year; probably had a final look at it together before I went off, in
some Gig, I think, to Crabbe's." He ends the letter with his translation of one of Omar's quatrains:

> I long for wine! oh Sáki of my Soul,
> Prepare thy Song and fill the morning Bowl;
> For this first Summer month that brings the Rose
> Takes many a Sultan with it as it goes.

He later changed the stanza to:

> And look—a thousand Blossoms with the Day
> Woke—and a thousand scatter'd into Clay:
> And this first Summer Month that brings the Rose
> Shall take Jamshýd and Kaikobád away.

By August 6, FitzGerald had a rough plan for a translation of the
Rubáiyát. "I see how a very pretty *Eclogue* might be tesselated out
of his scattered Quatrains," he wrote to Cowell; then, remembering
Cowell's religious scruples, he added, "but you would not like the
Moral of it. Alas!"[6] Cowell himself was at this time planning to
submit an article on Omar Khayyam to *Fraser's Magazine* which had
already published three articles by Cowell, including one on Jami,
but which had rejected FitzGerald's *Salámán and Absál.* On December 8, 1857, FitzGerald wrote to Cowell of his intentions regarding the Omar quatrains that he had translated:

You talked of sending a Paper about him to Fraser, and I told you, if you
did, I would stop it till I had made my Comments. I suppose you have not
had time to do what you proposed, or are you overcome with the Flood of
bad Latin I poured upon you? Well: don't be surprised (*vext*, you won't be)
if *I* solicit Fraser for room for a few Quatrains in English Verse, however—
with only such an Introduction as you and Sprenger give me—very short—
so as to leave you to say all that is Scholarly if you will. I hope this is not very
Cavalier of me. But in truth I take old Omar rather more as my property
than yours: he and I are more akin, are we not? You see all his Beauty, but
you don't feel *with* him in some respects as I do. I think you would almost

feel obliged to leave out the part of Hamlet in representing him to your Audience: for fear of Mischief. Now I do not wish to show Hamlet at his maddest: but mad he must be shown, or he is no Hamlet at all. G. de Tassy eluded all that was dangerous, and all that was characteristic. I think these *free* opinions are less dangerous in an old Mahometan, or an old Roman (like Lucretius) than when they are returned to by those who have lived on happier Food. I don't know what you will say to all this. However I dare say it won't matter whether I do the Paper or not, for I don't believe they'll put it in.

How correct FitzGerald was in his estimate of Cowell's approach—"you don't feel *with* him . . . as I do"—can be seen from Cowell's article on the Persian poet that was published in the *Calcutta Review* of March, 1858. Entitled, "Omar Khayyam, the Astronomer-Poet of Persia," it was a review of two works on Khayyam—of K. Woepke's 1851 Paris edition of Omar's *Algebra* and of the article "Khayyám" from A. Sprenger's catalog of the Oude collection of manuscripts. In Cowell's account of Omar, he included his translation of a number of the quatrains; his literal rendering of one of the stanzas reads

> Wheresoever is rose or tulip-bed,
> Its redness comes from the blood of kings;
> Every violet stalk that springs from the earth,
> Was once a mole on a loved one's cheek.

FitzGerald's version of the same quatrain illustrates dramatically the difference between translation and creation:

> I sometimes think that never blows so red
> The rose as where some buried Caesar bled;
> That every Hyacinth the Garden wears
> Dropt in its Lap from some once lovely Head.

Cowell's article on Omar Khayyam is interesting for two reasons. First, he was FitzGerald's teacher in Persian, but his views about Omar were not shared by FitzGerald. Second, his article represents the attitude of a Victorian Orientalist who is not untypical of his times when he expresses a distaste for all things not Christian and not English. He judges Khayyam not as a poet but as a heathen. In his opinion, Omar was not a mystic; his knowledge of the exact

sciences "kept him from the vague dreams of his contemporaries."
But Cowell thinks that Omar would have been better off had he
been a mystic: "The mysticism, in which the better spirits of Persia
loved to lose themselves, was a higher thing, after all, than his keen
worldliness, because this was of the earth, and bounded by the
earth's narrow span, while that, albeit an error, was a groping after
the divine."

Cowell sees a deep gloom in Omar's poetry and offers his reason
for it:

He lived in an age and country of religious darkness, and the very men
around him who most felt their wants and misery, had no power to satisfy or
remove them. Amidst the religious feeling which might be at work, acting
in various and arbitrary directions, hypocrisy and worldliness widely mingled; and every where pressed the unrecognised but yet over-mastering
reality—that the national creed was itself not based on the eternal relations
of things as fixed by the Creator. The religious fervour, therefore, when it
betook itself to its natural channel to flow in—the religion of the people—
found nothing to give it sure satisfaction; the internal void remained
unfilled.

Cowell compares Omar to Lucretius, but he thinks that "Omar
Khayyam builds no system,—he contents himself with doubts and
conjectures,—he loves to balance antitheses of belief, and settle
himself in the equipoise of the sceptic." In Cowell's view, "Fate and
free will, with all their infinite ramifications, and practical
consequences,—the origins of evil,—the difficulties of evidence—
the immortality of the soul—future retribution,—all these questions
recur again and again. Not that he throws any new light upon these
world-old problems, he only puts them in a tangible form, condens-
ing all the bitterness in an epigram." From this group of philosophical verses, Cowell selects what he calls "two of the more harmless";
for he thinks that some of the "most daring" are better left in the
Persian:

> I am not the man to fear annihilation;
> That half forsooth is sweeter than this half which we have;
> This life of mine is entrusted as a loan,
> And when pay-day comes, I will give it back.
>
> Heaven derived no profit from my coming hither,
> And its glory is not increased by my going hence;

> Nor hath mine ear ever heard from mortal man,—
> This coming and going—why they are at all?

Cowell's second stanza would be more familiar to readers in
FitzGerald's version:

> Into this Universe, and *why* not knowing,
> Nor *whence*, like Water willy-nilly flowing:
> And out of it, as Wind along the Waste,
> I know not *whither*, willy-nilly blowing.

Cowell's description of Omar's verses as "most daring" may seem
strange to present-day readers, but Omar's "impiety" was shocking
to many Victorians, and FitzGerald himself was aware of this reaction. Thomas Wright records in his biography an anecdote showing
FitzGerald's respect for the religious scruples of others. In 1882,
when he visited his childhood friend Mary Lynn, he gave her copies
of his *Sea Words and Phrases, Euphranor,* and other publications.
"Aware that Miss Lynn had no sympathy with the agnosticism in his
great poem, he said to her, 'I shall not give you a copy of *Omar
Khayyam,* you would not like it,' to which she said simply, 'I should
not like it.' 'He was very careful,' commented Miss Lynn,' 'not to
unsettle the religious opinions of others.' "[7]
Cowell's article on Omar Khayyam perhaps reveals more about
Cowell himself and the mores of his times than about Omar. The
deadly seriousness of Cowell's approach shows no comprehension of
Omar's humor and his light-heartedness—both so important to an
understanding of his poetry. FitzGerald, however, did appreciate
the humor in Omar and seems to have captured to a small extent his
tongue-in-cheek ridicule of convention. He did not regard Khayyam
as a mystic, as some other Orientalists did; and the many translators
who have tried to follow in FitzGerald's footsteps have adopted one
view or the other, depending on their own background. The
wrangle over what philosophical label to attach to Omar Khayyam
continues to this day. In 1858, Cowell summarized the reason for
Omar Khayyam's skepticism:

That Omar in his impiety was false to his better knowledge, we may readily
admit, while at the same time we may find some excuse for his errors, if we
remember the state of the world at that time. His clear strong sense re-
volted from the prevailing mysticism where all the earnest spirits of his age

found their refuge, and his honest independence was equally shocked by the hypocrites who aped their fervour and enthusiasm; and at that dark hour of man's history, whither, out of Islam, was the thoughtful Mohammedan to repair? No missionary's step, bringing good tidings, had appeared on the mountains of Persia. . . .

More than a hundred years after Cowell, a Soviet writer on Omar has found an entirely different reason for what he terms the "negativism" of Omar's philosophy. In his work *Khayyam*, A. Bolotnikov thinks that Omar, though a rebel, was unable to revolutionize the social conscience through his writings. Bolotnikov states that, since the world of commerce and finance to which Omar looked for support was unable to combat the feudal system, this defeat created the despairing skepticism in Omar that merges into a pessimism without hope. Cowell had sought an answer in religion, but the Soviet writer finds it in class struggle and in the failure of revolution. The only truth that emerges is the immortality of the genius of two men—Omar and FitzGerald—whose poems continue to hold the attention of readers and critics while times change and ideologies alter.

Even before the publication of Cowell's article in the *Calcutta Review*, FitzGerald had completed his translation of Omar's quatrains. In January, 1858, he gave it to J. W. Parker of *Fraser's Magazine*, who told him the magazine would publish thirty-five of the "less wicked" stanzas; but he told Parker that he might find them "rather dangerous among his Divines." *Fraser* kept the *Rubáiyát* for almost a year; but FitzGerald, who had gloomily predicted that the magazine would not print them, was not surprised. He wrote to Cowell that he supposed "they don't care about it: and may be quite right." He thought that, if the magazine did not publish his quatrains, he would copy them and send them to Cowell, adding, "My Translation will interest you from its *Form*, and also in many respects in its *Detail:* very unliteral as it is. Many Quatrains are mashed together: and something lost, I doubt, of Omar's Simplicity, which is so much a Virtue in him."[8]

By November, FitzGerald was sure that *Fraser's Magazine* had no intention of publishing his quatrains. "I really think I shall take it back," he wrote to Cowell on November 2, "add some Stanzas which I kept out for fear of being too strong; print fifty copies and give away; one to you, who won't like it neither. Yet it is most ingeniously tesselated into a sort of Epicurean Eclogue in a Persian Garden." FitzGerald added forty more quatrains to the thirty-five he took back from the magazine, and he had the *Rubáiyát* printed and bound in brown paper. Of the two hundred and fifty copies of the small volume he had printed, FitzGerald kept forty for himself: sent copies to Cowell, Donne, and George Borrow, the author of *The Romany Rye;* and turned over the remainder to Bernard Quaritch, the bookseller, from whom FitzGerald bought Oriental and other works. He instructed Quaritch to advertise Omar Khayyam in the *Athenaeum,* in any other paper he thought good, and to send copies to the *Spectator* and others. Enclosing payment for the advertisement and "any other incidental Expenses regarding Omar," FitzGerald wrote to Quaritch, "I wish him to do you as little harm as possible, if he does no good."[9]

Any satisfaction FitzGerald may have felt in the completion of his self-appointed task was soon marred by the death of his dear friend, W. K. Browne, who had been the model for Phidippus in *Euphranor.* Browne, who had been badly injured in a riding accident, lingered in great pain for several weeks. FitzGerald visited him and burst into tears when he heard Browne's familiar greeting, "My dear Fitz—old fellow" uttered in slow, painful syllables. "I went to see him before he died," FitzGerald wrote to Cowell on April 27, 1859. "the comely spirited Boy I had known first seven and twenty years ago lying all shattered and Death in his Face and Voice. . . . Well, this is so: and there is no more to be said about it. It is one of the things that reconcile me to my own stupid Decline of Life—to the crazy state of the world—Well—no more about it." Referring to the volume of the *Rubáiyát* that had been printed, he added:

I sent you poor old Omar who has *his* kind of Consolation for all these Things. I doubt you will regret you ever introduced him to me. And yet you would have me print the original, with many worse things than I have translated. The Bird Epic might be finished at once: but "cui bono?" No one cares for such things: and there are doubtless so many better things to care about. I hardly know why I print any of these things, which nobody buys; and I scarce now see the few I give them to. But when one has done one's best, and is sure that that best is better than so many will take pains to do, though far from the best that *might be done,* one likes to make an end of the matter by Print. I suppose very few People have ever taken such Pains in Translation as I have: though certainly not to be literal. But at all Cost, a Thing must *live:* with a transfusion of one's own worst Life if one can't retain the Original's better. Better a live Sparrow than a stuffed Eagle.

Here, in his own words, is FitzGerald's guiding philosophy in all his translations—a thing must live. He was slighted for not adopting a scholarly approach, and he was attacked for taking liberties with his originals. FitzGerald himself placed little value on his own works; whenever he referred to Omar, he included a little apology for the Persian's "wickedness." But his awareness of the opinions of others did not deter him from undertaking those tasks that he considered worthwhile. Even Cowell's lukewarm attitude towards the translations did not discourage FitzGerald greatly. Fortunately for English literature, FitzGerald adhered to his principle of "making an end of the matter by print." Though he always severely underrated his own efforts, and talked in 1859 of shutting up shop in the poetic line, he did continue his translations by rendering two more plays from Calderon into English, by adapting *Agamemnon* and the Oedipus dramas of Sophocles, and by putting the finishing touches to the *Bird-Parliament*, which he had hoped to print, but never did.

The story of the first edition of the *Rubáiyát* has been told many times. The small volumes stayed forgotten on Quaritch's shelves for a long time, and several were lost when the bookseller moved to new quarters. The copies that remained were marked down in price repeatedly, and they finally appeared in the penny box outside the shop. There they caught the eye of a contributing editor of the *Saturday Review*, believed to be Whitley Stokes, who purchased several copies at a penny each and distributed them among his friends. Someone, perhaps Stokes himself, mentioned the unusual quatrains to Gabriel Rosetti who told Algernon Swinburne about them. They bought copies for themselves; and, fascinated by what they read, returned to buy more copies. They found that the unexpected demand for the book had raised its price. The fame of the *Rubáiyát* soon spread among the Pre-Raphaelite brotherhood. Swinburne, Rosetti, and William Morris praised the book and distributed it among their friends. Swinburne gave a copy to Edward Burne-Jones, who showed it to John Ruskin in 1863. Ruskin was so impressed by the quatrains that he sat down immediately and wrote a note addressed to the translator of the *Rubáiyát of Omar Khayyám*, to be delivered when the identity of the poet should become known. This note remained with Burne-Jones for nearly ten years, for not until 1872, when the third edition of the *Rubáiyát* appeared, was FitzGerald identified as the translator of the *Rubáiyát*.

III *The Editions of the* Rubáiyát

The enthusiastic reception of the *Rubáiyát* by the Pre-Raphaelites stimulated demand, and by 1865 Quaritch was asking FitzGerald to consider a new edition. But FitzGerald, who had no financial interest in the venture and little hope of any literary success, could not make up his mind. His indecision seems to have been finally ended by praise from a dear friend. Mrs. Tennyson, who corresponded with FitzGerald, usually answering letters on her husband's behalf as well, wrote to him that Alfred Tennyson had expressed admiration for the *Rubáiyát*. FitzGerald was greatly pleased, and he embarked upon the task of preparing a second edition of the poem. To the seventy-five quatrains of the first edition, he added thirty-five more which increased the number of stanzas to one hundred and ten. He revised and altered many of the quatrains, and in some places changed their sequence.

In the preface to his first edition, FitzGerald had set forth the view that Omar Khayyam was not a Sufi and that his *Rubáiyát* did not propound mystical allegories. In 1867, J. B. Nicolas published the text of a lithograph copy of Khayyam's quatrains that he had found in Tehran, as well as a prose translation in French in which he stated his conviction that Omar was a Sufi whose songs of wine and pleasure carried hidden mystical meanings. FitzGerald studied Nicolas' volume while preparing his second edition; and though he found inspiration in it for some new stanzas, he discovered no justification for the Frenchman's views, and no reason to alter his own opinion that Omar Khayyam was above all things a philosopher, as FitzGerald had stated in his preface to the first edition:

It has been seen that his Worldly Desires, however, were not exorbitant; and he very likely takes a humourous pleasure in exaggerating them above that Intellect in whose exercise he must have found great pleasure, though not in a Theological direction. However this may be, his Worldly Pleasures are what they profess to be without any Pretense at divine Allegory: his Wine is the veritable Juice of the Grape: his Tavern, where it was to be had: his Sáki, the Flesh and Blood that poured it out for him: all which, and where the Roses were in Bloom, was all he profess'd to want of this World or to expect of Paradise.

The second edition of the *Rubáiyát*, consisting of two hundred copies, was printed and put on sale in 1868. FitzGerald kept a few copies for himself to give to friends. FitzGerald's agreement of sale with Quaritch showed FitzGerald's lack of interest in any financial gain. The bookseller was empowered to fix a salable price for the books; to take his own profit; and, after fifty copies were sold, to give the translator his share of the profits. FitzGerald would have handed the whole edition over to Quaritch to do with as he pleased had he not thought that he would "look more of a Fool by doing so." He did not expect even fifty copies to sell during his lifetime, and he remarked jokingly that his ghost would have to call upon Bernard Quaritch to collect his share of the profit.

The second edition of the *Rubáiyát*, with a hundred and ten stanzas, was the largest of all the five editions. In the third edition, FitzGerald cut back the *Rubáiyát* to a hundred and one stanzas; and he kept the fourth edition, the last one published in his lifetime, to the same length. Some of the stanzas that FitzGerald added to the second edition are as fine as the best of the first edition, as for example stanza 71, which does not appear in the first edition:

> I sent my Soul through the Invisible,
> Some letter of that After-life to spell:
>   And after many days my Soul return'd
> And said, "Behold, Myself am Heav'n and Hell:"

and stanza 72:

> Heav'n but the Vision of fulfill'd Desire,
> And Hell the Shadow of a Soul on fire,
>   Cast on the Darkness into which Ourselves,
> So late emerg'd from, shall so soon expire.

FitzGerald revised many of the stanzas of the first edition and changed the sequence of some of them. In each of the four editions and in the fifth one as well, which was published after his death, there are alterations and revisions, sometimes only a word or two in a stanza. FitzGerald did not refer to the original in making these changes, for his objective was not to bring his version closer to the Persian but to please his own fastidious literary judgment. The famous "Book of Verses" in the stanza that is the eleventh in the first edition, twelfth in the second, and the twelfth in the subsequent three editions—shows his method of revision:

1859

Here with a Loaf of Bread Beneath the Bough,
A Flask of Wine, a Book of Verse—and Thou
  Beside me singing in the Wilderness—
And Wilderness is Paradise enow.

1868

Here with a little Bread beneath the Bough
A Flask of Wine, a Book of Verse—and Thou
  Beside me singing in the Wilderness—
Oh, Wilderness were Paradise enow!

1872

A Book of Verses underneath the Bough,
A Jug of Wine, a Loaf of Bread—and Thou
  Beside me singing in the Wilderness—
Oh, Wilderness were Paradise enow!

1879 and 1889

A Book of Verses underneath the Bough,
A Jug of Wine, a Loaf of Bread—and Thou
  Beside me singing in the Wilderness—
Oh, Wilderness were Paradise enow!

FitzGerald's later revisions did not please many of those who had
admired the first edition, among them A. C. Swinburne, who
thought that the first edition was the only one worth having since
FitzGerald had deleted from the later editions the first stanza which
Swinburne considered the crowning stanza, the core or kernel of the
whole work. In the first stanza in the first edition, FitzGerald is
closer to the original than in the subsequent editions; he employs in
it Omar's images of the emperor of day who is casting the pebble
into the cup to signal the start of the chase, and the sun is throwing
the noose of morning upon the rooftops:

    Awake! for Morning in the Bowl of Night
    Has flung the Stone that puts the Stars to Flight.
      And Lo! the Hunter of the East has caught
    The Sultán's Turret in a Noose of Light.

In the second edition of 1868 FitzGerald altered this stanza to read:

> Wake! For the Sun behind yon Eastern height
> Has chased the Session of the Stars from Night;
> And, to the field of Heav'n ascending strikes
> The Sultan's Turret with a Shaft of Light.

In the 1872 edition he changed it again:

> Wake! For the Sun who scatter'd into flight
> The Stars before him from the Field of Night,
> Drives Night along with them from Heav'n, and strikes
> The Sultán's Turret with a Shaft of Light.

In the fourth and fifth editions, he left the stanza in its 1872 form and only added a comma after "Sun" in the first line. FitzGerald obviously preferred the later version, but many a reader would agree with Swinburne that the first version is the best.

The second edition of 1868 also did not bear the translator's name, but Quaritch seems on occasion, to have conveniently forgotten FitzGerald's wish for anonymity. In Quaritch's catalog of books that was issued in the autumn of 1868, E. FitzGerald, Esq., was listed as the translator of Omar Khayyam. The advertisement did not escape FitzGerald's notice, for he wrote to Quaritch that the price of three shillings and six pence for a copy of the *Rubáiyát* made him blush.

Meanwhile, the fame of the *Rubáiyát* had spread to the United States. In 1868, Charles Eliot Norton, an American critic and writer, who was a frequent visitor to England, was shown the *Rubáiyát* by his friend Burne-Jones, who also told Norton about John Ruskin's note addressed to the anonymous translator. Norton carried back to the United States a copy of the second edition of the *Rubáiyát* as well as the translation in French by J. B. Nicolas. Using the two versions as the basis of his review, Norton published an article in the *North American Review* of October, 1869, in which he was enthusiastic in his praise of FitzGerald's *Rubáiyát;* he considered FitzGerald's work not so much a translation as a literary masterpiece in its own right:

He is to be called "translator" only in default of a better word, one which should express the poetic transfusion of a poetic spirit from one language to another, and the re-presentation of the ideas and images of the original in a form not altogether diverse from their own, but perfectly adapted to the new conditions of time, place, custom, and habit of mind in which they reappear. In the whole range of our literature there is hardly to be found a more admirable example of the most skilful poetic rendering of remote foreign poetry than this work of an anonymous author affords. It has all the merit of a remarkable original production, and its excellence is the highest testimony that could be given, to the essential impressiveness and worth of the Persian poet. It is the work of a poet inspired by the work of a poet; not a copy, but a reproduction, not a translation, but the redelivery of a poetic inspiration.

At the end of the review, Norton quoted seventy-six of FitzGerald's quatrains. Norton's article, the first review of the *Rubáiyát* to appear in any periodical, firmly established the reputation of the poem in the United States. The number of readers increased steadily, much to FitzGerald's surprise, who had predicted an "immortality" of a dozen years for his book. It was mostly to satisfy the demand of admirers in the United States that the third and fourth editions of the *Rubáiyát* were published.

In England, however, FitzGerald's *Rubáiyát* continued to be ignored by the critics until 1870 when *Fraser's Magazine* at last took notice of the poem. In the June issue of that year, an unsigned review of the *Rubáiyát* was published by the periodical. The reviewer, who later identified himself in a letter to Quaritch as Thomas W. Hinchliff, took notice of the difference in approach between the French version of the *Rubáiyát* by Nicolas and the English version. The reviewer, who congratulated the anonymous English translator on the "excellence and elegance of his performance," declared that "it would be difficult to find a more complete example of terse and vigorous English, free from all words of weakness or superfluity." The reviewer devoted eight pages to the poem in which he retraced the historical background of Omar and quoted Norton's tribute to the *Rubáiyát* in the *North American Review*. In a comparison which seems forced, the British reviewer tried to establish a similarity between Tennyson and Omar by quoting lines from *In Memoriam* and *The Two Voices* to prove his point. He maintained that the lines from *The Two Voices*—

> To Which he answered scoffingly;
> Good Soul! suppose I grant it thee,
> Who'll weep for *thy* deficiency?

> Or will one beam be less intense,
> When *thy* peculiar difference
> Is cancelled in the world of sense?

—expressed sentiments akin to Omar's:

> And fear not lest existence closing *your*
> Account, should lose, or know the type no more;
>   The eternal Saki from that bowl has poured
> Millions of bubbles like us, and will pour.

> When you and I behind the veil are past,
> Oh but the long long while the world shall last,
>   Which of our coming and departure heeds
> As much as ocean of a pebble-cast.

The writer's conclusion was in favor of Tennyson's philosophy as opposed to Omar's:

It is the scepticism of a man, who, after working through all the fields of science open to him, finds himself disposed to weep despairingly over the unsatisfactory result of human knowledge. Tennyson, in the masterly poem alluded to, was as unable as Omar to untie the knot in a logical manner; but, with the better light of modern thought to guide him, he cut it by an assertion of faith in the beauty and life and happiness of the world around him. To the old Persian sage such a lofty stage of thought was perhaps impossible: he knew the difficulty equally well, but he was not prepared with such a happy solution of it. We must be content to admire his verses for their intrinsic beauty. The vigour of his thought and expression, and their harmony with much that is now going on around us, inspire us with a strange feeling of sympathy for him who in the darkest ages of Europe filled himself with all knowledge accessible to him before he went to his last sleep under the roses of Naishápúr.

Though FitzGerald was pleased with the favorable review, he still did not think that the *Rubáiyát* would attract many readers. He wrote to Quaritch on July 8, 1870:

Thank you for your note about poor old Omar's first *"fiasco"*—I suppose he does not fare much better now, in spite of all those Gentlemen's good opinions; which might not have been the case had one of them given him a good word years ago. But I never *ask* anyone to do such a Job for me, as

someone I hear has now done in Fraser's Magazine. However Omar does
not take up much room on your shelves, & will go off one day—when
probably I shall be out of reach of a third Edition of 150 copies. Meanwhile I
console myself with my little ship, & am
                                        Yours truly, Edward FitzOmar.

FitzGerald, of course, could not have been more wrong. Not only
was the fame of his *Rubáiyát* becoming well-established across the
Atlantic, but the name of the translator as well, largely unknown in
England, was no secret to a circle of Omarians in the vicinity of
Philadelphia. Mrs. Sarah Wister, the daughter of FitzGerald's old
friend Fanny Kemble, was acquainted with FitzGerald's writings;
and she was certain that FitzGerald was the translator of the
Rubáiyát. She wrote to him, and was pleased to learn that she had
guessed correctly. Thus, while *Fraser's Magazine* was paying tribute
to the anonymous English translator of Omar Khayyam, Horace H.
Furness, the Shakespeare scholar, was writing to Quaritch from
Philadelphia in December, 1870: "If you ever communicate with
Mr. Edward FitzGerald, I wish you would express to him, if he care
to learn it, the keen delight with which his translation has been read
by quite a circle of my friends here in this city; and I must confess so
exquisite is the English and rhythmical is the verse that we all,
ignorant as we are of the original, mistrust that the beauties of Omar
are largely due to the genius of the translator."[10]
    Owing largely to the purchases of admirers such as Furness, who
bought ten copies of the *Rubáiyát*, the second edition of 1868 was
almost completely sold. Quaritch, who did not wish to lose this
modestly lucrative business with customers across the Atlantic, was
trying to persuade FitzGerald to prepare a new edition by dovetail-
ing the first and second editions. But FitzGerald's eyes were bother-
ing him, and he was reluctant to undertake any extensive alterations. Moreover, he did not like Quaritch's suggestion of "reconcil-
ing two in one"; he thought that "such a scheme, with brackets &c.
would be making too much of the thing: and you and I might both be
laughed at for treating my Omar as if it were some precious frag-
ment of Antiquity." His own plan was to have the second edition
republished, "with some Whole Stanzas which may be 'de trop' cut
out, & some of the old readings replaced." He added the following
note to the letter, which is dated March 31, 1872: "By the by,
Cowell wrote me some months ago that Ed^{n}1 had been reprinted by

someone in India. So I have lived not in vain, if I have lived to be
Pirated!" The date of the letter, March 31, coincided with
FitzGerald's birthday; and FitzGerald notes it: "Easter Sunday my
own Birthday (64). I wonder how it is with Omar but I think I
know."

After the third edition of the *Rubáiyát* was published in 1872,
FitzGerald wrote to Quaritch on August 24: "I found Omar on my
return home yesterday. I can only say that I doubt you have put him
into a finer Dress than he deserves—and that some other Critics will
have their Bile raised to say so—if they take any notice now of the
old Offender. I only hope you have not overestimated your Transat-
lantic friends who I fancy are our chief Patrons—the Americans (as I
found from Mrs. Wister—a daughter of Mrs. Kemble's) taking up a
little *Craze* of this sort now and then." As for FitzGerald's share of
the profit from the second edition, he instructed Quaritch to give it
to some charity, public or private: "If the Persian *Famine Fund* still
subsists, the money might properly be added to that—as I daresay
old Omar would have done—had he translated the Works of yours
truly." From the third edition, FitzGerald asked for a dozen copies
for himself; and bound copies were sent to Cowell and to Alfred
Tennyson. His own copies FitzGerald wanted "*not* bound, as I
would do them up with a Revision of Salámán which I amused
myself with two years ago. So I can stitch up the Saint & the Sinner
together, for better or for worse." Obviously, FitzGerald had not
forgotten *Salámán*, Cowell's favorite and his own: and remembered
it again when the time came for a fourth edition of the *Rubáiyát*.

Just as the second edition with its revisions and additions had
displeased some admirers of the first edition, the third edition with
its alterations drew protest from at least one admirer of the second
edition. Thomas Hinchliff wrote a letter to Quaritch dated January
28, 1876, in which he not only identified himself as the writer of the
review in *Fraser's Magazine* but also expressed his disappointment
with the changes in the third edition and the increase in price:

When I sent for the copy of Omar Khayyám for which I am sorry to see that
I have forgotten to pay, it was for the purpose of sending it to a friend whose
acquaintance I made when in Japan, & one I knew would appreciate it. I am
honest enough to tell you that when I found it had grown at a jump from half
a crown to 7s 6d I looked over it to see what changes there might be in the
text, in company with my friend Mr. Simpson, the artist of the Illustrated

News now in India, who is another worshipper of Omar: but we were grieved to find that Mr FitzGerald, in altering the text here and there, had grievously injured the Original. So much so that we agreed to send our friend in Japan an old copy which I had to spare, instead of the new and smarter edition. In quatrain 12 and in the last few of the poem I think the changes have been peculiarly for the worse, and regret it deeply. The old edition was so good that I should have liked to see "well let alone." Authors however will have their own fancies on such points.

Though the third edition was published mainly for the American market, the *Rubáiyát* was gaining readers in England, and curiosity about its authorship was increasing. Norton, who was visiting England in 1872, heard it rumored that the translator of the *Rubáiyát* was a certain Reverend Edward FitzGerald who lived somewhere in Norfolk and was fond of boating. The following spring, while walking with his friend Thomas Carlyle, Norton mentioned the *Rubáiyát* and expressed his admiration for it. Carlyle remarked that he had never heard of the poem, and asked whose work it was; Norton repeated to him what he had heard—that the translation was by a Reverend Edward FitzGerald who lived in Norfolk and who spent much time in his boat. Norton relates Carlyle's reaction:

The Reverend Edward FitzGerald?" said he in reply. "Why, he's no more Reverend than I am! He's a very old friend of mine. . . . I'm surprised, if the book be as good as you tell me it is, that my old friend has never mentioned it to me"; and then he went on to give me a further account of FitzGerald. I told him I would send him the book, and did so the next day. Two or three days later, when we were walking together again, he said: "I've read that little book which you sent to me, and I think my old friend FitzGerald might have spent his time to much better purpose than in busying himself with the verses of that old Mohammedan blackguard." I could not prevail on Carlyle even to do credit to the noble English in which FitzGerald had rendered the audacious quatrains of the Persian poet; he held the whole thing as worse than a mere waste of labour.[11]

Norton remarks in another place that Carlyle had not taken to Omar Khayyam because he had found Omar's skepticism too blank and his solution of life in drink too mean. To Norton, "Carlyle's talk about Omar . . . was the Philistinism of a man of genius."[12]

When Norton informed Burne-Jones about his discovery of the translator's identity, he was sent Ruskin's letter with the request that it be given to the author of the *Rubáiyát*. Norton enclosed the letter in a note to Carlyle, saying that, "if he would not object to giving FitzGerald pleasure, on the score of his translation of the verses of the 'old Mohammedan blackguard,' " he was to put the right address on the letter and forward it to the translator. Carlyle sent both the note and Ruskin's letter to FitzGerald; and, in spite of his strictures against Omar, he added a handsome tribute of his own. He called FitzGerald's translation "excellent," and "the Book itself a kind of jewel in its way." FitzGerald wrote his thanks to Norton in a letter of April 17, 1873:

Two days ago Mr. Carlyle sent me your Note, enclosing one from Mr. Ruskin "to the Translator of Omar Khayyám." You will be a little surprized to hear that Mr. Ruskin's note is dated September 1863: all but ten years ago! I dare say he had forgotten all about it long before this: however, I write him a Note of Thanks for the good, too good, messages he sent me; better late than never; supposing that he will not be startled and bored by my Acknowledgments of a forgotten Favor rather than gratified. It is really a funny little Episode in the Ten years' Dream.

FitzGerald's letter was the beginning of an epistolary friendship with Norton which lasted until FitzGerald's death.

Ruskin's letter, which was dated September 2, 1863, read as follows:

My dear and very dear Sir,

I do not know in the least who you are, but I do with all my soul pray you to find and translate some more of Omar Khayyam for us: I never did—till this day—read anything so glorious, to my mind as this poem—(10th. 11th. 12th pages if one were to choose)—and that, and this, is all I can say about it—More—more—please more—and that I am ever gratefully and respectfully yours.

J. Ruskin.[13]

The popularity of the *Rubáiyát*, especially among the Americans, "Omar's best Friends," as FitzGerald called them, was increasing the sales of the book; and by 1875 Quaritch was hinting about another edition. But FitzGerald did not think that there would be enough demand to justify a fourth edition. He did concede, however, that Omar had done better than he had expected: "As to old Omar—I think he has done well, considering that he began his En-

glish Life as an 'Enfant Trouvé'—or rather 'perdu' in Castle Street
15 years ago. I only wonder he has survived up to this time. We will
leave at present to smoulder away what Life is in him—perhaps as
much as in myself. I had once wished to associate him with the
Jámi—which I altered, but which I suppose no one would care for
with all my alterations—"[14] While Quaritch was still discussing the
feasibility of another edition, Boston publisher James Osgood issued
a reprint of the third edition in 1878. FitzGerald, who was sent a
copy of the volume, wrote to Quaritch about it on January 25, 1878:
"I know not if I am in any way indebted to you for a handsome—too
handsome—Edition of Omar which came here a week ago; Messrs.
Osgood, I see, Publishers. I wish that, at any rate, they would have
let me know of their intention, as I have a few alterations, & an
additional Note."

FitzGerald wrote again to Quaritch two days later about the Osgood reprint: "I think Messrs. Osgood who are, I believe, respectable Publishers, might have apprized me before they brought out
their Edition. It is such a Curiosity of spinning out that I will send it
to you to look at. But I think I will, as I said, leave Omar for the
present; there has been Enough of him here, & now will be more in
America. One day I may bring him out in better Company." The
better company was *Salámán and Absál* which FitzGerald hoped to
rescue from obscurity. He had hinted at this long-cherished wish
when the second edition of the *Rubáiyát* was published; and he had
even bound the third edition of the *Rubáiyát* with the revised edition of *Salámán*, a few copies of which FitzGerald had had printed at
Ipswich. But Quaritch chose not to take the hint.

When the American reprint of the *Rubáiyát* appeared, Quaritch
urged the necessity of another edition; but FitzGerald, whose
Agamemnon had been printed in 1876, had no wish to undertake
another revision of the *Rubáiyát*. He had, however, set his heart on
introducing *Salámán* to Omar's ever-increasing readers; and he told
Quaritch that the only condition upon which he would agree to a
fourth edition of Omar was that *Salámán* be included with the
Rubáiyát. He did not wish *Salámán* to be printed separately, as
Quaritch proposed to do. "Salámán however would be much longer,
& not half so welcome," he wrote to Quaritch on August 19, 1878,
"& that is why I did not think he w^d do alone. Besides, I really could
not bear another of my things to be separately published, & recommended by Advertisement, so close upon the other two: whereas,

alongwith Omar for Trumpeter, Salámán might come modestly forth: *both*, at a moderate price. *You*, however, may wish to keep the two separate; and that much you can tell me about if you care to do so; and I will then decide what shall be done in this very important matter." Quaritch had no desire to saddle the popular favorite with the unknown *Salámán*. But FitzGerald remained adamant. He did say, however, that he would consult with Cowell on the subject and let Quaritch know his decision. "If Omar be reprinted, Cowell wishes Salámán to go along with him," FitzGerald announced in his next letter of December 9, 1878; and Quaritch had to surrender.

The fourth edition of the *Rubáiyát*, in company with the revised *Salámán and Absál*—my "Persian Siamese" as FitzGerald called them—was published in 1879. The book was to have been dedicated to Cowell, but it finally appeared without any dedication. Cowell, according to FitzGerald, was "frightened at last from the two which he taught me being dedicated to him, as he had once agreed to: & even wished for." FitzGerald took an unusual amount of interest in the form and size of the volume, and he lavished a great deal of care on the printing of *Salámán*. Convinced that this edition would be the last one in his lifetime, FitzGerald made certain stipulations, the first of which was that "Omar, who is to stand *first*, be never printed separate from Jami."[15] He hoped in this way to ensure that *Salámán* would not be forgotten as long as the *Rubáiyát* was remembered. FitzGerald's affection for *Salámán and Absál*, if misplaced, is still understandable. *Salámán* was associated with his friend Cowell and a pleasant era in FitzGerald's life, as he himself admitted. FitzGerald also had great respect for Cowell's scholarship; and, modest and unassuming as FitzGerald was, he must have felt pride in Cowell's approval of his translation of *Salámán and Absál*.

But personal reasons alone cannot account for FitzGerald's preference for *Salámán*. He was too meticulous an artist to have included *Salámán* with the *Rubáiyát* if he had had any doubts about the literary quality of the former. His reasons for insisting upon having both published together must have been literary as well as personal. From the moral point of view, Omar would appear, especially to a contemporary of FitzGerald, as a debauched spokesman for cynicism and godlessness. FitzGerald himself leaned towards agnosticism, but he was not a professed atheist. He did not regard Omar as a heathen wandering in the outer darkness; and, though he included quotations from Cowell in his preface, he did not agree with Cowell's "apology" for Omar. Nor did he consider Omar's praises of wine an indication of the poet's debauchery. He might have realized, however, that many of his readers would not agree with him; for, not having read the Persian, they would not only consider Omar an advocate of immorality, but would identify FitzGerald with this attitude. *Salámán*, on the other hand, represents a higher, spiritual view of life. Its allegory attaches a deeper meaning to life than the "eat, drink, and be merry" philosophy of the English *Rubáiyát*. The presence of the moral *Salámán* would nullify, therefore, the effect of the epicurean Omar.

Placing *Salámán and Absál* side by side with the *Rubáiyát* may also have been FitzGerald's way of answering those Orientalists who maintained that Omar Khayyam was a Sufi. Jami's mysticism is undisputed and his *Salámán and Absál* is regarded as a true mystical allegory. By reading both *Salámán* and the *Rubáiyát*, it would be possible to see not only what true mysticism was, but also how different from it was the imagery of the *Rubáiyát*. Philosophically and artistically, *Salámán* offers a perfect balance to the *Rubáiyát*. The latter ends on a note of resignation; whatever religion may have to say about the immortality of the soul, there could be no rebirth for man as far as observation and reason tell the poet. In *Salámán*, the ending is a glorious justification of faith. In the *Rubáiyát*, man descends into earth to become a part of it; in *Salámán*, man ascends to heaven to become one with the Deity. The shining light in the concluding lines of *Salámán* is in direct contrast to the "night" quatrains of the *Rubáiyát*. The *Rubáiyát* sings of the body; *Salámán* of the soul. FitzGerald knew that Omar spoke for him and for all mankind, but he may not have wished to leave Omar as his only spokesman. When the reader judged him, the mystic was to be there with the skeptic. Whether or not FitzGerald had all these objectives in view, he obviously failed in his effort to raise *Salámán* to the eminence that the *Rubáiyát* was soon to occupy in the hearts of millions all over the world. FitzGerald's emphatic stipulation that Omar never be published without *Salámán* was apparently disregarded after his death. His wish that "perhaps Persian, Greek, and Spanish might one day all gather into one little Volume" did not materialize in his own lifetime. Nor did he live to see the "little Craze" of the *Rubáiyát* grow into a worldwide popularity that has outlasted the works of contemporaries FitzGerald himself regarded as towering geniuses.

IV *FitzGerald's Version of the* Rubáiyát

FitzGerald's *Rubáiyát*—the "Epicurean Eclogue" as FitzGerald once described it—follows a pattern that is lacking in the original. By their very genre, Omar Khayyam's quatrains are individual entities that formulate and present a complete idea in each stanza and follow no set arrangement. The Persian manuscripts that FitzGerald used for his translation had the quatrains arranged in an alphabetical order, a method often used for the convenience of both the copyist and the reader. The *rubai*, the Persian word for the quatrain, is regarded as a typically Iranian innovation. According to a popular story, the rhythm of the *rubai* was discovered by a Persian poet in the ninth or tenth century who used as his metrical model a phrase sung by a boy at play. The lyrical swing of the *rubai* and its short and epigrammatic form soon made it a popular vehicle of poetic expression among both the common folk and the literati. To compose a *rubai* on the spur of the moment became a skill worthy of respect and a pastime indulged in by the quick witted and the fluent.

The *rubai* consists of four hemistichs of up to thirteen syllables each, and a rhyme scheme of *a a b a* or *a a a a*. Traditionally, the first three hemistichs are regarded as the prelude to the fourth, which should be sublime, subtle, or epigrammatic. The range of subject matter and the variation of thought and mood in the *rubai* are unlimited; masters of the poetic art as well as anonymous composers of folk poetry have used the form. Sometimes, the masters have indulged in the ribald as well as in the sublime—the contrast one finds in the quatrains of Omar Khayyam. The obscene jests in some of his stanzas greatly perplexed and troubled Omar's French translator J. B. Nicolas, who nevertheless stoutly maintained that Omar was a Sufi who employed only mystical imagery in his quatrains.

As regards the authenticity of the stanzas attributed to Omar in the manuscripts that have come under scholarly scrutiny, including the two manuscripts that FitzGerald used as his sources, no consensus exists among Orientalists. Some scholars, mostly in the West, have questioned the authorship of many of the quatrains and have attributed them to anonymous poets, but others have seen no reason to doubt that Khayyam composed the stanzas bearing his name. The process of authentication has been rendered difficult by the fact that no manuscripts of the *Rubáiyát* are to be found either in

Khayyam's own hand or with his signature. The fact that no manuscripts survive from Omar's own lifetime, or from the period after his
death is undoubtedly the result of the havoc wrought by the Mongol
invasion which destroyed a large part of the cultural wealth of Iran.

Selections from Khayyam's *Rubáiyát*, however, have appeared in
Persian anthologies, one of which goes as far back as 1611. These
anthologies attest to the popularity of Omar's *Rubáiyát* and the
existence of a large number of his quatrains at one time. No one who
has read Omar's *Rubáiyát* in Persian can deny their merit. Khayyam
may not be in the first rank of Persian poets, but he is not among the
least. Persian scholars regard him as a liberal agnostic in the tradition of Avicenna and as a forerunner of Hafez in whose poetry
Omar's earthly wine assumes a mystical significance. Omar's place
in the hierarchy of poets is expressed best in a statement attributed
to the Moghul Emperor of India, Akbar, who said that each of
Hafez's *ghazals* ("lyrics") should be accompanied by a *rubai* from
Omar Khayyam, for reading Hafez without Omar was like wine
without relish.

As for the philosophical content of FitzGerald's *Rubáiyát*, the
diversity of thought in the Persian original far outstrips that of the
English version. Omar's quatrains are not confined to the themes of
doubt of a future life and the advocacy of enjoyment in this one. The
freedom of the *rubai* form allowed Omar to indulge in satire,
parody, veiled jokes sometimes taken as serious observations by
critics, and in piety as well as skepticism. His changes of mood are
one reason for his popularity, for every man can find a corroboration
of his own state of mind in Omar.

The parodoxes of life that Omar points out in his *Rubáiyát* have
puzzled men for centuries. Sufism was one attempt to answer these
questions. The Sufi movement started in the early years of Islam,
perhaps in the seventh or eighth century, and gained many adher-
ents. The word Sufi is derived from the Arabic word *suf* and denotes
an individual who prefers to wear a garment of simple woollen cloth
rather than the silks and brocades fashionable among the wealthy.
The Sufis renounced worldly goods and physical comforts, and devoted their lives to seeking reunion with the Creator. In its heyday
in Iran, Sufism inspired some of the finest poems in the Persian
language. The movement, however, fell into disrepute, and some of
its practices drew sharp criticism not only from orthodox Muslims
who regarded Sufism as dangerously close to heresy, but also from
intellectuals in general.

Some of Omar's *rubais* enunciate thoughts found in Sufism, thus leading to the theory that Omar was a Sufi. Those who hold this view, however, disregard Omar's attacks on the hypocrisy of the Sufis and his jokes at their expense. His works show him to have been a liberal philosopher who tried to examine questions in the light of reason and logic. If his musings sometimes sound like mysticism or Sufism, it may be because mysticism also tries to find reasons for ostensibly unreasonable phenomena; and in its attempts to do so, it sometimes resorts to logical absurdities. As a creed, Sufism has rigidities that an independent thinker like Omar would have found hard to accept; nor is it possible to believe that a rationalist like Omar could have subscribed to the extremes of thought and behavior practiced by the Sufis in general.

FitzGerald himself described Omar in his preface to the *Rubáiyát* as a man "of such moderate worldly Ambition as becomes a Philosopher, and such moderate wants as rarely satisfy a De-bauchee," who bragged more than he drank of the wine that he celebrates. If FitzGerald had been better acquainted with the conventions of Persian poetry, he might have pointed out as well that the wine mentioned with such frequency in Omar's poetry could be regarded as one of these conventions. Since wine was forbidden by Islam, it came to be used as a symbol of many things, such as rebellion against fate, the forbidden fruit, the hope of future happiness—since holy wine is one of the joys provided in paradise—and the mystical love of God. Persian poets have used wine in innumerable contexts; and, if they have praised it not symbolically but for its earthly effects, they have refrained from saying so openly, perhaps hoping that the nondrinker would interpret their wine as a symbolic one, and the wine-drinker embrace them as a comrade in sin. The wisdom of this course is illustrated by Omar's *Rubáiyát*, which is accepted by one group as mystical and by another as a celebration of inebriety.

Omar uses wine in many contexts, sometimes as a device to illustrate the absurdities in human concepts of sin and virtue. Khayyam is always critical of convention, but his attitude is not that of an indignant social reformer, but that of a scholar with a sense of humor. His approach is a tongue-in-cheek one, and his verses are lighthearted. He cannot resist applying the principles of logic and mathematics to all conventional beliefs, including the poetic and religious. In one quatrain, he examines addiction to wine in the light of the belief in divine omniscience. God knew, he says, since the

beginning of time, that Omar would drink wine. If Omar should not
drink wine, would it not turn God's omniscience to ignorance? Obviously an impossibility!

In another *rubai*, Omar propounds a joke in logic. His opponents
told him, he says, not to drink, because wine is the enemy of faith.
Realizing this, Omar declares, I swore by God that I would drink
the blood of the enemy; for killing the enemies of God is a forgivable
act. Drinking then, by Omar's calculation, becomes a doubly
meritorious action. He is not above poking fun at the Deity; and, in
one quatrain that is popular among the Persians, he complains that
God had broken his jug of wine and ruined his pleasure. Dear God,
he asks, could it be that you are drunk? Omar may or may not have
written this stanza himself; but this irreverent humor is so typical of
his quatrains that one can easily believe that Omar wrote it.

Little of Khayyam's humor survives in the English version.
Perhaps FitzGerald did not understand or could not capture in
English the subtle jokes, and the ribald and irreverent ones he left
alone. He did notice the concepts of logic, mathematics, and physics
that Omar employs in his *rubais*. In a note to stanza fifty-six in the
third and fourth editions, he points out that the lines were a jest at
his studies. He says that Omar has a mathematical quatrain compar-
ing himself and his beloved to a pair of compasses, a metaphor made
famous in English poetry by John Donne.

Omar's observations on life that have earned him the reputation
of skeptic can be reduced to a few essential points. He advocates
that man make the most of this life; for, whatever sages and saints
may say, no one has verified the existence of another world beyond
this one. He poses the question of sin and evil; if God created the
world and everything in it, he also created evil. The responsibility
for the existence of evil in this world thus lies at God's own door.
Since only good emanates from God, wine and sin cannot be evil, for
these are also God's creations.

V *FitzGerald's Innovations*

In regard to FitzGerald's *Rubáiyát*, the reader who is unac-
quainted with the Persian may still find it hard to decide whether
FitzGerald's poem is a translation or mostly his own creation. Persian words such as "Máh" and "Máhi" and the names of Persian
monarchs that are deliberately used by FitzGerald to give an Oriental color to his poèm tend to confuse the student, who begins to

search for abstruse Eastern allusions in quatrains that proclaim their meaning in plain English. To look for obscurity in FitzGerald's *Rubáiyát* is to defeat the poet's main objective in not only the quatrains but in all his poems: the presentation of a foreign or difficult concept in a form familiar to the English reader. As FitzGerald repeatedly said in his letters, he was trying to achieve literary excellence rather than fidelity to the original. In this pursuit of excellence, he achieved in the *Rubáiyát* a lyrical beauty that in places outstrips the Persian.

Since FitzGerald conceived of the *Rubáiyát* as an "Epicurean Eclogue," he chose from Khayyam only those quatrains that fitted this pattern. He discarded all those stanzas that expressed piety or religious sentiment, though he was well aware of them; for in a letter to George Borrow of June, 1857, he copied the Persian and translated one of Khayyam's quatrains expressing repentance:

> Alas, that life is gone in vain!
> My every mouthful is unlawful, every breath is tainted;
> Commands not fulfilled have disgraced me;
> And alas for my unlawful deeds!

In choosing to translate only the "epicurean" quatrains, FitzGerald gave the *Rubáiyát* a superficiality and a one-sidedness not found in the original. On the other hand, FitzGerald's English version sparkles with a sustained light and color found only occasionally in the Persian. FitzGerald seems to have captured in his *Rubáiyát* the sunlight and spring flowers of his beloved Suffolk, all the more precious because so fragile and transient. Like the paradox of life itself, the poem evokes visions of beauty while constantly reminding one of its evanescence; FitzGerald's quatrains cluster around the single theme of the shortness of life and the uncertainty of the future. As he said many times, his poem is intended for those who are not acquainted with the Persian; for such a reader does not then miss the many subtle meanings and allusions in Khayyam's quatrains, and he does not resent FitzGerald's treatment of the Persian. To appreciate the *Rubáiyát*, one should regard it, therefore, as an English poem inspired by a Persian poet.[16]

FitzGerald's contribution to the shaping of the *Rubáiyát* is evident in the form of the English version. In the Persian, each independent quatrain expresses a thought and a mood perhaps quite different from the preceding or the succeeding one. In composing his version, FitzGerald had to find a unifying element which would connect the stanzas to each other and form a continuous whole. He solved the problem by introducing the element of drama and by giving his poem the unity of time—one day; the unity of character—the poet himself; and the unity of action—the poet's musings.

FitzGerald explained his approach in the *Rubáiyát* in a letter he wrote to Quaritch on March 31, 1872, in which he was defending the alterations and additions in the second edition which had displeased some readers:

I daresay Ed[n] 1 is better in some respects than 2, but I think not altogether. Surely, several good things were added—perhaps too much of them which also gave Omar's thoughts room to turn in, as also the Day which the Poem occupies. He begins with Dawn pretty sober and contemplative: then as he thinks & drinks, grows savage, blasphemous &c., and then again sobers down into melancholy at nightfall. All which wanted rather more expansion than the first Ed[n] gave. I dare say Ed[n] 1 best pleased those who read it first: as first Impressions are apt to be strongest.

The introduction of action in a poem which deals essentially with philosophical concepts was a difficult task that FitzGerald accomplished successfully. He chose as his opening stanza a quatrain which does not appear as the first one in either of the two sources that he used. The quatrain conveys a sense of urgency and propels the reader into the dramatic action:

> Awake! for Morning in the Bowl of Night
> Has flung the Stone that puts the Stars to Flight:
> And Lo! the Hunter of the East has caught
> The Sultán's Turret in a Noose of Light.

The journey of the sun across the sky, of man in this life, and of Omar through the realm of philosophy is on its way. The second and third stanzas maintain the hurried, breathless pace set by the first quatrain, and they convey the basic concept of the poem—that, in this life, there is no time to postpone pleasure. In the fourth edition, FitzGerald specified that the first three stanzas, which he called the "Lever de Rideau," should appear on the first page.

The start of day also heralds the advent of springtime in the fourth stanza:

> Now the New Year reviving old Desires,
> The thoughtful Soul to Solitude retires,
>   Where the WHTE HAND OF MOSES on the Bough
> Puts out, and Jesus from the Ground suspires.

For the poet, spring is the time of youth and pleasure; "The Nightingale cries to the Rose," and the poet calls out for more wine (Seventh stanza):

> Come, fill the Cup, and in the Fire of Spring
> The Winter Garment of Repentance fling:
>   The Bird of Time has but a little way
> To fly—and Lo! the Bird is on the Wing.

The three succeeding stanzas all continue the imagery of spring. Stanza eight introduces summer:

> And look—a thousand Blossoms with the Day
> Woke—and a thousand scatter'd into Clay:
>   And this first Summer Month that brings the Rose
> Shall take Jamshýd and Kaikobád away.

Stanzas nine to thirteen continue the images of early summer—green herbage, red rose, blossoms of a thousand hue. The twelfth stanza is the famous "Here with a Loaf of Bread beneath the Bough," and the quatrains of early summer culminate in the exquisite thirteenth:

> Look to the Rose that blows about us—"Lo,
> "Laughing," she says, "into the World I blow:
>   "At once the silken Tassel of my Purse
> "Tear, and its Treasure on the Garden throw."

The fourteenth stanza creates an abrupt change with its "Ashes" and its "Snow upon the Desert's dusty Face." The fifteenth stanza, however, returns to the summer images of golden grain, rain, wind, and aureate earth. FitzGerald apparently did not like the break in continuity, for in the second edition he inserted the "Golden grain" stanza after that of "the blowing Rose"; and he also made the "Ashes" quatrain number seventeen and the prelude to stanzas suggesting a change in mood, season, and the time of day.

In the first edition, stanzas sixteen to twenty-two indicate a change from early summer. The absence of color in these quatrains, the repeated use of "day," the description of Bahram sleeping, and the loveliest and the best drinking a round or two and creeping silently to rest—all evoke a quiet and somnolent atmosphere such as prevails at high noon in midsummer. Stanza twenty-two, which mentions summer's dressing in new bloom, gives an indication of the season of the year the poet is still describing. The section seems to end with the twenty-third stanza, which introduces a series decrying abstract theorizing. Even in quatrains that deal with abstract concepts, FitzGerald maintains the lively and energetic pace by using active metaphors, as in stanza twenty-eight:

> With them the seed of Wisdom did I sow,
> And with my own hand labour'd it to grow:
> And this was all the Harvest that I reap'd—
> "I came like Water, and like Wind I go."

Images that occur most frequently in the *Rubáiyát* are the rose, the nightingale, and the green of spring and summer, all of which are favorite topics of Persian poetry. FitzGerald also uses light and color to indicate the time of day and the change of seasons, as well as to evoke a mood. Stanzas twenty-three, twenty-four, and twenty-five, which describe the futility of conjectures about the future, emphasize darkness and dust:

> Ah, make the most of what we yet may spend,
> Before we too into the Dust descend;
> Dust into Dust, and under Dust, to lie,
> Sans Wine, sans Song, sans Singer, and—sans End!

> Alike for those who for To-Day prepare,
> And those that after a TO-MORROW stare,
> A Muezzín from the Tower of Darkness cries
> "Fools! your Reward is neither Here nor There!"

> Why, all the Saints and Sages who discuss'd
> Of the Two Worlds so learnedly, are thrust
> Like foolish Prophets forth; their Words to Scorn
> Are scatter'd, and their Mouths are stopt with Dust.

Stanzas twenty-nine and thirty ask the reason for man's creation in lines that flow with the sharpness of a clear mountain spring:

> Into this Universe, and *why* not knowing,
> Nor *whence*, like Water willy-nilly flowing:
> And out of it, as Wind along the Waste,
> I know not *whither*, willy-nilly blowing.

> What, without asking, hither hurried *whence?*
> And, without asking, *whither* hurried hence!
> Another and another Cup to drown
> The Memory of this Impertinence!

Because these stanzas are as colorless as water, the brilliant flash of stanza thirty-one comes as a surprise:

> Up from Earth's Centre through the Seventh Gate
> I rose, and on the Throne of Saturn sate,
> And many Knots unravel'd by the Road;
> But not the Knot of Human Death and Fate.

The seventeen stanzas that follow concentrate primarily on the play of light and shadow: Destiny's Lamp and "little Children stumbling in the Dark" (stanza 33); "Dusk of Day" in the marketplace (36); the stars setting and the caravan starting for the "Dawn of Nothing" (38); "The Angel Shape" stealing through the dusk (42); the "black Horde" contrasted with the polish of the "enchanted Sword"(44); and the "Magic Shadow-show/Play'd in a Box whose Candle is the Sun" (46). The only touches of color in these stanzas are gold, rose, and ruby vintage; and each is mentioned only once. The tempo of the poem quickens suddenly in stanza forty-nine, and is heightened in stanza fifty by the metaphor of the player striking the ball. The action reaches a peak in stanzas fifty-four and fifty-five, which together form a complete sentence:

> I tell Thee this—When, starting from the Goal,
> Over the shoulders of the flaming Foal
>   Of Heav'n Parwin and Mushtara they flung,
> In my predestin'd Plot of Dust and Soul

> The Vine had struck a Fibre; which about
> If clings my Being—let the Súfi flout;
>   Of my Base Metal may be filed a Key,
> That shall unlock the Door he howls without.

These two stanzas, and stanza fifty-six, all of which contain words of
light, heat, and suddenness, suggest to the mind's eye the last brilliant light cast by a sinking sun. Stanza fifty-eight with its direct
address to the Deity—

> Oh, Thou, who Man of baser Earth didst make,
> And who with Eden didst devise the Snake;
>   For all the Sin wherewith the Face of Man
> Is blacken'd, Man's Forgiveness give—and take!

—provides a fitting end to the day and to the start of night which, as
FitzGerald may or may not have known, is observed by Omar's
countrymen with a prayer.

Stanza fifty-nine, which in the first edition is the beginning of the
"Kúza-Náma" or the episode of the pots, uses the storyteller's device of attracting his audience's attention, "Listen again," in order to
set the stage for the dramatic narrative of the pots. The episode
occupies that part of the evening when the sun has set, but the
moon has not as yet risen. The haze of twilight which surrounds the
stanzas is skillfully suggested by "the surly Tapster," his visage
daubed with the "smoke of Hell." The greyness of twilight is
matched, as it were, with the aridity of abstract speculation in stanza
sixty-five:

> Then said another with a long-drawn Sigh,
> "My Clay with long oblivion is gone dry:
>   "But, fill me with the old familiar Juice,
> "Methinks I might recover by-and-by!"

The advent of "the little Crescent" ends the episode and ushers in a
mood of calm cheerfulness. The garden is alive again; perfume is in
the air; spring has come; and nature has renewed herself. But, for
the poet, there is no return. His farewell is sad, but not bitter:

> Ah, with the Grape my fading Life provide,
> And wash my Body whence the Life has died,
>   And in a Windingsheet of Vine-leaf wrapt
> So bury me by some sweet Garden-side.

> That ev'n my buried Ashes such a Snare
> Of Perfume shall fling up into the Air,
>   As not a True Believer passing by
> But shall be overtaken unaware.

Though the poet is no more, he lives on in nature, having merged with it.

The end of the poem returns to the beginning: the garden, spring, and wine. But, in place of the hubbub of dawn, there is the peaceful quiet of a moonlit night. The last two stanzas of the *Rubáiyát* shine with a lyrical beauty seldom matched in English literature:

> Ah, Moon of my Delight who know'st no wane,
> The Moon of Heav'n is rising once again:
> How oft hereafter rising shall she look
> Through this same Garden after me—in vain!

> And when Thyself with shining Foot shall pass
> Among the Guests Star-scatter'd on the Grass,
> And in thy joyous Errand reach the Spot
> Where I made one—turn down an empty Glass!

VI *Kúza-Náma*

In the episode of the pots, FitzGerald retained the paradoxes formulated by Omar. FitzGerald arranged the speculative stanzas consecutively in the form of questions. In the 1872 edition, he revised one of the stanzas to indicate the Sufistic nature of the questions raised. In the first edition, he had written the stanza thus:

> And, strange to tell, among that Earthen Lot
> Some could articulate, while others not:
> And suddenly one more impatient cried—
> "Who *is* the Potter, pray, and who the Pot?"

(stanza 60)

In the second edition he revised the stanza:

> Thus with the Dead as with the Living, *What?*
> And *Why?* so ready, but the *Wherefor* not,
> One on a sudden peevishly exclaim'd,
> "Which is the Potter, pray, and which the Pot?"

(stanza 94)

This version did not please FitzGerald, for in the third edition he changed it, adding the word "Súfi" as well"

> Whereat some one of the loquacious Lot—
> I think a Súfi pipkin—waxing hot—

> "All this of Pot and Potter—Tell me, then,
> "Who makes—Who sells—Who buys—Who *is* the Pot?"
>
> (stanza 87)

In the fourth edition, he restored the last line to its original form, but left the first three lines intact:

> Whereat some one of the loquacious Lot—
> I think a Súfi piplin—waxing hot—
> "All this of Pot and Potter—Tell me, then,
> "Who is the Potter, pray, and who the Pot?"
>
> (stanza 87)

In the first edition, the questions appear under "Kúza-Náma," beginning with stanza sixty, and ending with the rising of the crescent, stanza sixty-six. FitzGerald arranges them in succession: (A) What is the true nature of existence, and of man's relationship to God? (B) If God created man for a purpose, why does he stamp him back to earth again? Why does God create beautiful things, and then destroy them for no apparent reason? (C) If there is ugliness, why did God create it? (D) If God is all-merciful, would it not be against his nature to punish men? Stanza sixty-five offers no solution, but a way of escape from exhausting and insoluble paradoxes—the old familiar juice of the grape which at least ensures a jolly time while life lasts.

In later editions, FitzGerald removed the subtitle of "Kúza-Náma," or the episode of the pots; but he left the questions arranged consecutively and as parts of the episode. In the second edition, FitzGerald added a number of stanzas with a philosophical content, perhaps influenced by his reading of Nicolas' edition of the *Rubáiyát* from the manuscript he had found in Iran. The sequence of stanzas fifty to fifty-five of the second edition are not in the first edition. Stanza thirty-six, which first appears in the second edition, draws upon an allusion in Attar's *Mantic uttair*, which FitzGerald also translated, for the image of the mourning sea:

> Earth could not answer; nor the Seas that mourn
> In flowing Purple, of their Lord forlorn;
>   Nor Heav'n, with those eternal Signs reveal'd
> And hidden by the sleeve of Night and Morn.

Since FitzGerald allowed himself great latitude in composing the English version of the *Rubáiyát,* allusions appear from his other readings, both Oriental and non-Oriental. He was fully aware of the common heritage of Eastern and Western thought, and he pointed out in a note to the *Rubáiyát* the occurrence of the metaphor of the Potter and the Pot in different literatures of the world. Thus he did not consider it improper to add a dash of Calvinism to Omar's Persian philosophy in stanza fifty-seven of the first edition:

> Oh, Thou, who didst with Pitfall and with Gin
> Beset the Road I was to wander in,
>   Thou wilt not with Predestination round
> Enmesh me, and impute my Fall to Sin?

Or even to contribute his own philosophy in the famous epigrammatic line of stanza fifty-eight:

> Oh, Thou, who Man of baser Earth didst make,
> And who with Eden didst devise the Snake;
>   For all the Sin wherewith the Face of Man
> Is blacken'd, man's Forgiveness give—and take!

CHAPTER 5

Spanish, Greek, and Persian

I More Translations from Calderon

BEFORE embarking upon the translation of the *Rubáiyát*, FitzGerald had planned to translate three dramas, Calderon's *El Mágico Prodigioso* and *La Vida es Sueño*, and *Agamemnon* by Aeschylus. FitzGerald had first been attracted to Calderon by these two plays; but he had refrained from "meddling" with them on the grounds that they were among the dramatist's masterpieces. He had chosen, instead, six of Calderon's lesser known plays. After the publication of the *Six Dramas*, however, he did try translating the two plays; but he laid them aside when the results did not please him. In 1864, he resumed work on the plays again, inspired, he said, perhaps by Cowell's return from India. When he rewrote the two plays, he molded them into a shape of his own choosing, so that, as he wrote to Cowell, "scarce a Plank remains of the original! Pretty impudence: and yet all done to conciliate English, or modern, Sympathy. This I shan't publish: so say (pray!) nothing of it at all—remember—only I shall print some Copies for you and one or two more: and you and Elizabeth will like it a great deal too much. There is really very great Skill in the Adaptation, and Remodelling of it."

As for the changes he had made in *El Mágico Prodigioso*, he explained: "I cut out all the precioso very ingeniously: and give all the Mountain-moving, etc., in the second Act without Stage direction, so as it may seem to pass only in the dazzled Eyes, or Fantasy, of Cyprian. All this is really a very difficult Job to me; not worth the Candle, I dare say: only that you two will be pleased. I also increase the religious Element in the Drama; and make Cyprian outwit the Devil more cleverly than he now does; for the Devil was certainly too clever to be caught in his own Art. *That* was very good Fun for an Autodafé Audience, however."[1]

Two words of the motto now filch'd are enough
For the impudent mixture they label—such stuff!

The story centers around Segismund, the son of Basilio, the king of Poland. Before Segismund's birth, his father had read in the stars that the child would one day create strife in the land and depose his father. To prevent this forecast, Basilio had kept Segismund imprisoned in a dungeon and ignorant of his royal birth. The death of the queen at Segismund's birth obviously had not softened Basilio's feelings toward his son. At the time the play opens, Segismund is a young man who realizes the wretchedness of his plight but cannot understand the reason for it. By an improbable accident, he meets Rosaura, a Muscovite lady, who, with her attendant Fife, has come to Poland in search of Astolfo, the duke of Muscovy and nephew to Basilio. The duke was to have married Rosaura, but he had broken his word when Basilio had offered him the throne of Poland, which he would rule jointly with his cousin, Princess Estrella.

Before relinquishing his throne to Estrella, his niece, and to Astolfo his nephew, Basilio decides to give Segismund one last chance to prove that the prophecy was wrong. He is to be brought to the palace while asleep under the influence of drugs, and he is to be addressed as prince and heir to the throne. If he should behave with restraint and courtesy, then Basilio is to surrender the kingdom to him and retire; if he should prove savage and vengeful, then he is to be returned to the dungeon for life. The king's orders are carried out, and Segismund is brought to the palace and told the secret of his birth. The prince, overcome with bitterness, becomes violent; and King Basilio orders that he be drugged and returned to prison. Prince Segismund is finally rescued by a band of soldiers who rebel against the king's unjust punishment of his son. Led by Rosaura, they engage the king's forces in battle and are victorious. Given a second chance, Segismund proves himself a wise and merciful prince, and succeeds to his father's throne with the old man's blessings. He announces his betrothal to Estrella, and Rosaura's engagement to Astolfo, and the play ends on a happy note.

Although FitzGerald seems to have had doubts about his work in *Such Stuff as Dreams Are Made Of*, in literary quality it approaches his best efforts. The blank verse flows with unfettered ease; the play occasionally scintillates with passages of great lyrical beauty and emotional impact, as in this poignant lament by Segismund, and

Rosaura's reply, the pathos of which is heightened by the repeated "Alas":

Seg.   Oh, think, if you who move about at will,
        And live in sweet communion with your kind,
        After an hour lost in these lonely rocks
        Hunger and thirst after some human voice
        What must one do where all is mute, or harsh,
        And ev'n the naked face of cruelty
        Were better than the mask it works beneath?—
        Across the mountain then! Across the mountain!
        What if the next world which they tell one of
        Be only next across the mountain then,
        Though I must never see it till I die,
        And you one of its angels?
Res.   Alas! Alas!
        No angel! And the face you think so fair,
        'Tis but the dismal frame-work of these rocks
        That makes it seem so; and the world I come from—
        Alas, alas, too many faces there
        Are but fair vizors to black hearts below,
        Or only serve to bring the wearer woe!
        But to yourself—if haply the redress
        That I am here upon may help to yours.
        I heard you tax the heav'ns with ordering,
        And men for executing, what, alas!
        I now behold. But why, and who they are
        Who do, and you who suffer—
Seg.   (pointing upwards). Ask of them,
        Whom, as to-night, I have so often ask'd,
        And ask'd in vain.

FitzGerald's effective use of repetitive words and phrases is also illustrated in the following exchange between Clotaldo and Segismund. Clotaldo, the warden of the dungeon, is trying to convince Segismund that his experiences of the night before at his father's palace were nothing more than a dream. Clotaldo's sober poetry is punctuated with Segismund's musical refrain of "last night, last night"; Clotaldo uses the metaphor of the eagle in flight, a favorite one of FitzGerald's:

Clo.   Such dreams
        Are oftentimes the sleeping exhalations

Of that ambition that lies smouldering
Under the ashes of the lowest fortune;
By which when reason slumbers, or has lost
The reins of sensible comparison,
We fly at something higher than we are—
Scarce ever dive to lower—to be kings,
Or conquerors, crown'd with laurel or with gold,
Nay, mounting heav'n itself on eagle wings.
Which, by the way, now that I think of it,
May furnish us the key to this high flight—
That royal Eagle we were watching, and
Talking of as you went to sleep last night.

Seg.   Last night? Last night?

Clo.   Ay, do you remember
Envying his immunity of flight,
As, rising from his throne of rock, he sail'd
Above the mountains far into the West,
That burn'd about him, while with poising wings
He darkled in it as a burning brand
Is seen to smoulder in the fire it feeds?

Seg.   Last night—last night—Oh, what a day was that
Between that last night and this sad To-day!

In this same scene, FitzGerald presents two contrasting soliloquies—one serious, the other humorous—on the theme, life is a
dream. Clotaldo reflects philosophically on the illusory nature of
life; Fife contributes his own comments on Clotaldo's soliloquy, and
illustrates the theme of illusion with his own adventures since coming to Poland in the company of his mistress Rosaura, who is dis-
guised as a boy:

Clo.   So sleep; sleep fast: and sleep away those two
Night potions, and the waking dream between
Which dream thou must believe; and, if to see
Again, poor Segismund! that dream must be.—
And yet, and yet, in these our ghostly lives,
Half night, half day, half sleeping, half awake,
How if our waking life, like that of sleep,
Be all a dream in that eternal life
To which we wake not till we sleep in death?
How if, I say, the senses we now trust
For date of sensible comparison,—
Aye, ev'n the Reason's self that dates with them,

Should be in essence or intensity
Hereafter so transcended, and awoke
To a perceptive subtilty so keen
As to confess themselves befool'd before,
In all that now they will avouch for most?
One man—like this—but only so much longer
As life is longer than a summer's day,
Believed himself a king upon his throne,
And play'd at hazard with his fellows' lives,
Who cheaply dream'd away their lives to him.
The sailor dream'd of tossing on the flood:
The soldier of his laurels grown in blood:
The lover of the beauty that he knew
Must yet dissolve to dusty residue:
The merchant and the miser of his bags
Of finger'd gold; the beggar of his rags:
And all this stage of earth on which we seem
Such busy actors, and the parts we play'd,
Substantial as the shadow of a shade,
And Dreaming but a dream within a dream!

Fife's wry soliloquy, which follows Clotoldo's, provides a moment of
light comedy before the start of the action—the battle between the
troops supporting the prince and the king's soldiers:

Fife.   Such talk of dreaming—dreaming—I begin
To doubt if I be dreaming I am Fife,
Who with a lad who call'd herself a boy
Because—I doubt there's some confusion here—
He wore no petticoat, came on a time
Riding from Muscovy on half a horse,
Who must have dreamed she was a horse entire,
To cant me off upon my hinder face
Under this tower, wall-eyed and musket-tongued,
With sentinels a-pacing up and down,
Crying All's well when all is far from well,
All the day long, and all the night, until
I dream—if what is dreaming be not waking—
Of bells a-tolling and processions rolling
With candles, crosses, banners, San-benitos,
Of which I wear the flamy-finingest,
Through streets and places throng'd with fiery faces
To some back platform—
Oh, I shall take a fire into my hand

> With thinking of my own dear Muscovy—
> Only just over that Sierra there,
> By which we tumbled headlong into—No-land.
> Now, if without a bullet after me,
> I could but get a peep of my old home—
> Perhaps of my own mule to take me there—
> All's still—perhaps the gentlemen within
> Are dreaming it is night behind their masks—
> God send 'em a good nightmare!—Now then—Hark!
> Voices—and up the rocks—and armèd men
> Climbing like cats—Puss in the corner then.

Fife's own dream ends when he is shot in the battle and dies.

II *Translation of Aeschylus*

While preparing the two Calderon dramas for printing, FitzGerald had at first thought of including his version of *Agamemnon* but had then decided against it. He had sketched his translation of the play in 1857, but he had laid it aside with the hope of eventually returning to it with fresh eyes and trimming it into shape. That day seems to have come finally in 1869 when, at Mrs. Kemble's urging, he put the finishing touches to the manuscript and had a hundred copies printed by Childs. He tried to keep the translation a secret by asking Cowell, to whom he sent a copy, not to "leave it about." But the play was soon discovered; for W. H. Thompson, FitzGerald's friend and the Master of Trinity College, had requested a volume of FitzGerald's works for the library and found *Agamemnon* among the translations. In the United States, Mrs. Kemble's friends who had heard of the play from her, were writing to Quaritch to ask for copies. Quaritch in turn applied to FitzGerald and at first received half a dozen copies of the play to be given away free. But Quaritch not only sold the copies, but also advertised *Agamemnon* in his catalog under FitzGerald's name, much to FitzGerald's distress and indignation:

Surely you must have misunderstood me about those few Agamemnons. Surely I distinctly wrote along with them that they were to be *given* to any American who troubled himself to ask for them, as two or three have done before—just to save further trouble to all Parties. And now a cutting from one of your Catalogues has [been] sent me announcing the Play for sale—at some terrible price for such a Scrap—and moreover *with my Name*, which I had always declined publishing—and such a Puff about me and my little

works as I am really ashamed to read again. It is quite true that I might
someday, if there was likely to be any demand, have published the Play,
and some Calderon: but I am quite sure I never asked you to put the few
Copies I sent you up to sale.[2]

The remainder of the one hundred volumes, which FitzGerald
turned over to Quaritch, were soon gone, and Quaritch urged
FitzGerald to prepare a second edition. By the middle of January,
1876, FitzGerald had revised the play and sent it to Quaritch. Two
hundred and fifty copies were published, anonymously, at
FitzGerald's insistence; he did not want his name mentioned because he thought there were too many FitzGeralds, none of them
celebrated except the lord of that name. "Why, there is one beside
myself in this very Woodbridge, an Ex-policeman," he wrote to
Quaritch; "there lately was another, a Parson, in a neighbouring
Village; you knew another to your Cost," referring to a book thief by
the name of FitzGerald. "In fact one of us was generally hanged in
Ireland once a Year till the law was altered—Shall all these dispute
my Glory?" he asked dramatically.[3]

The translator's name, however, did not remain a secret for long;
nor was Agamemnon ignored as FitzGerald's earlier works had
been. "Why haven't you sent us 'Agamemnon,' " the editor of The
Academy enquired of Quaritch in February; "here is Mr. Symonds
waiting to review it along with Omar Khayyám." Even before
Symonds' review appeared in The Academy, an American periodical, The Nation of New York had published on May 24, 1877, a
critique of the Agamemnon. The reviewer had praise for FitzGerald,
but he tempered it with criticism of his handling of certain portions
of the play. "The grander soliloquies and descriptions in the
'Agamemnon' have never been so well rendered," the reviewer
declared; "we may almost say that they have never before been
rendered at all." After the reviewer had quoted from the scene in
which Cassandra is brought before Clytemnestra, he observed that
"There is no scene in Macbeth of more tremendous power; and
although all this, as here quoted, is rather a transfusion than a
translation, yet it gives more of the real sense of the original than all
previous translations put together."

While praising FitzGerald's rendering of the stirring and
dramatic passages, the reviewer expressed disappointment at Fitz-
Gerald's inability to do justice to the more delicate and tender

descriptions, some of which FitzGerald had omitted altogether. The reviewer's final verdict, however, was a flattering one: "It would be safest to say that this remarkable poem is not to be placed in the department of translations, but rather of original works, and that it is Greek only in the sense in which Keats's 'Hyperion' is Greek, or the sublime audacities of Marlowe, whose mighty genius touched the self-same ancient theme of love and wrong." FitzGerald's comment on the review was that it was discriminating in its distribution of blame and praise.

In the issue of July 7, 1877, *The Academy* had similar praise for the play. In his review, John Addington Symonds accorded *Agamemnon* "a place apart among all English versions of Greek poetry." Remarking that it might be almost trivial to say that the diction of a modern author was Shakespearean, Symonds wrote:

Yet Mr. FitzGerald's style in the finest passages of this great torso has a weight, a compactness, and a picturesqueness, to find the proper parallel for which we must look back to Shakespeare's age. The strong sonorous verse has the richness and the elasticity of Marlowe's line; and for the first time, after so many attempts, the English reader catches in his translation a true echo of the pompous Aeschylean manner. . . . The result is that, while the whole poem is profoundly penetrated with the Aeschylean spirit, which it reproduces with wonderful vividness, and while certain portions are accurate transcripts from the original, the Greek student will find many of the most impressive passages suppressed, and some most carefully prepared effects omitted. . . . The language throughout the drama, even in the passages which may seem to have been injured by compression, is so grandiose, and the imagery is so Aeschylean, that it is impossible not to regret the author's disinclination to grapple with the Greek more closely. Where he has adhered to the original most faithfully, as in Clytemnestra's description of the courier fire, and her reception of Agamemnon, the success has been so thorough as to make us feel that the whole drama might have been presented with equal force and splendour. Is it quite beyond hope that Mr. FitzGerald should reconsider his decision and complete the play upon the strictly Aeschylean outlines? . . . In a word the most perfect portions of the tragedy are those which represent the Greek with most fidelity; the modern poet proving his ability to bear the whole Titanic weight if he had chosen, by the energy which he has disposed of certain favoured passages. . . . In conclusion, it may be permitted to hope that this *Agamemnon* is only the first of a series; and that the poet who possesses such rare powers of reproductive and re-creative translation may trust them so far upon another trial as to render his original in all its fullness.

Symonds' praise surprised FitzGerald, for he had translated *Agamemnon* not for Greek scholars but for those who did not know the original. In his introduction to the play, FitzGerald was explanatory and apologetic about his version, or his "per-version," as he called it: "I suppose that a literal version of this play, if possible, would scarce be intelligible. Even were the dialogue always clear, the lyric Choruses, which make up so large a part, are so dark and abrupt in themselves, and therefore so much the more mangled and tormented by copyist and commentator, that the most conscientious translator must not only jump at a meaning, but must bridge over a chasm; especially if he determine to complete the antiphony of Strophe and Antistrophe in English verse."

The lyric choruses posed the greatest problem for FitzGerald who did not consider himself enough of a poet to do them justice; he devised his choruses as a sort of "Entr'acte Music" which was to express the mood of the message of the Aeschylean group. He repeated this opinion in a note to the preface of his first edition of *Agamemnon:* "As for my Lyric Choruses—I wish the reader who does not know the Original (and this Version is scarcely for those who do) would but take the Subject, and supply, or supplant, my descant upon it from some such music as he may find in Beethoven, who breathes Aeschylus in his language as I cannot in mine." Though FitzGerald modestly called his choruses "mostly 'rot' quod poetry," great dramatic vigor appears in the exchanges between the chorus and the protagonists. This strength is particularly evident in the last portion of the play in which the music reaches a crescendo in the sharp reproofs traded between Aegisthus and the chorus and then subsides into calmness in Clytemnestra's concluding speech:

Chorus

Aegisthus, only creatures of base breed
Insult the fallen; fall'n too, as you boast,
By one who plann'd but dared not do the deed.
This is your hour of triumph. But take heed;
The blood of Atreus is not all outrun
With this slain King, but flowing in a son,
Who, saved by such an exile as your own
For such a counter-retribution—

Aegisthus

Oh,
You then, the nether benchers of the realm,
Dare open tongue on those who rule the helm?
Take heed yourselves; for, old and dull of wit,
And harden'd as your mouth against the bit,
Be wise in time; kick not against the spurs;
Remembering Princes are shrewd taskmasters.

Chorus

Beware thyself, bewaring me;
Remembering that, too sharply stirred,
The spurrer need beware the spurred;
As thou of me; whose single word
Shall rouse the City—yea, the very
   Stones you walk upon, in thunder
Gathering o'er your head, to bury
Thee and thine accomplice under!

Aegisthus

Raven, that with croaking jaws
   Unorphean, undivine,
After you no City draws;
   And if any vengeance, mine
Upon your wither'd shoulders—

Chorus

   Thine!
Who daring not to strike the blow
Thy worse than woman-craft design'd,
To worse than woman—

Aegisthus

Soldiers, ho!

Clytemnestra

Softly, good Aegisthus, softly; let the sword that has so deep
Drunk of righteous Retribution now within the scabbard sleep;

And if Nemesis be sated with the blood already spilt,
Even so let us, nor carry lawful Justice into guilt.
Sheath your sword; dismiss your spears; and you, Old
  men, your howling cease,
And, ere ill blood come to running, each unto his home in peace,
Recognizing what is done for done indeed, as done it is,
And husbanding your scanty breath to pray that nothing more amiss.
Farewell. Meanwhile, you and I, Aegisthus, shall deliberate,
When the storm is blowing over, how to settle House and State.

FitzGerald's version of *Agamemnon* achieves the clarity and the
sustained dramatic interest that was FitzGerald's reason for taking
liberties with the original: "If it has succeeded in shaping itself into a
distinct, consistent, and animated Whole, through which the reader
can follow without halting, and not without accelerating interest
from beginning to end, he will perhaps excuse my acknowledged
transgressions, and will not disdain the Jade that has carried him so
far so well till he find himself mounted on a Thorough-bred whose
thunder-clothed neck and long-resounding pace shall better keep
up with the Original." One easily forgives FitzGerald's avowed
transgressions when reading passages such as the following one,
where he adds his poetic imagination to the original's exhortation
"Call not on death," and produces an eloquent quatrain:

> Call not on Death, old man, that, call'd or no,
>   Comes quick; nor spend your ebbing breath on me,
>   Nor Helena: who but as arrows be
> Shot by the hidden hand behind the bow.

Other passages in the play arrest the eye and echo in the memory.
In this one, Menelaus is dreaming of Helen:

> At last the sun goes down along the bay,
> And with him drags detested Day.
> He sleeps; and, dream-like as she fled, beside
> His pillow, Dream indeed, behold! his Bride
> Once more in more than bridal beauty stands;
> But, ever as he reaches forth his hands,
> Slips from them back into the viewless deep,
> On those soft silent wings that walk the ways of sleep.

And this quatrain reflects sadly on fate:

> But thus it is; All bides the destined Hour;
> And Man, albeit with Justice at his side,
> Fights in the dark against a secret Power
> Not to be conquer'd—and how pacified?

III *Plays of Sophocles*

FitzGerald intended to translate as well *The Libation-bearers* and *The Furies*, thus completing the entire trilogy; but he only wrote a draft of the *Choephori* which he said he had reduced almost to an act. He did not finish it, and it was never printed. At the time he was writing *Agamemnon*, he had also sketched in his fashion Sophocles' *Oedipus Tyrannus* and *Oedipus Coloneus*. The manuscript lay unfinished until 1878 when his American friend C. E. Norton heard of it and asked for a copy. FitzGerald promised to send it to him, but he did not do so until Norton asked him again a year later. In a letter of September 3, 1879, FitzGerald was apologetic for the delay:

I laid the Plays by after looking them over some months ago, meaning to wait till another year to clear up some parts, if not all. Thus do my little works arrive at such form as they result in, good or bad; so as, however I may be blamed for the liberties I take with the Great, I cannot be accused of over haste in doing so, though blamed I may be for rashness in meddling with them at all. Anyhow, I would not send you any but a fair MS. if I sent MS. at all; and may perhaps print it in a small way, not to publish, but so as to ensure a final Revision, such as will also be more fitting for you to read. It is positively the last of my Works! having been by me these dozen years, I believe, occasionally looked at. So much for that.

By 1880, FitzGerald had completed his version of the two Sophocles plays; and he had united them into one drama of two parts. The first part dealt with Oedipus in Thebes; the second, with Oedipus at Athens. FitzGerald had the first part printed and sent to Norton on March 4, 1880. "I really hope you will like it, after taking the trouble more than once to ask for it," he wrote to Norton; "only (according to my laudable rule of Give or Take in such cases) say no more of it to me than to point out anything amenable: for which, you see, I leave a wide margin, for my own behoof as well as my reader's. And again I will say that I wish you would keep it wholly to yourself: and, above all, not let a word about it cross the Atlantic."

FitzGerald explained his approach in the translation:

> You will see at once that it is not even a Paraphrase, but an Adaptation, of the Original: not as more adapted to an Athenian Audience 400 years B. C. but to a merely English reader 1800 years A. D. Some dropt stitches in the Story, not considered by the old Genius of those days, I have, I think, "taken up,"·as any little Dramatist of these Days can do: though the fundamental absurdity of the Plot (equal to Tom Jones according to Coleridge!) remains; namely, that Oedipus, after so many years reigning in Thebes as to have a Family about him, should apparently never have heard of Laius' murder till the Play begins. One acceptable thing I have done, I think, omitting very much rhetorical fuss about the poor man's Fatality, which I leave for the Action itself to discover; as also a good deal of that rhetorical Scolding, which, I think, becomes tiresome even in its Greek: as the Scene between Oedipus and Creon after Tiresias: and equally unreasonable. The Choruses which I believe are thought fine by Scholars, I have left to old Potter to supply, as I was hopeless of making anything of them; pasting, you see, his "Finale" over that which I had tried.[4]

FitzGerald completed the second part of the Oedipus drama a year later and sent it to Norton along with a prefatory letter addressed to Norton's first initial, for, as FitzGerald explained, "I did not wish to compromise you even with yourself in such a Business." He added in his letter of March 13, 1881, "I know you will like it probably more than it deserves, and excuse its inroads on the Original, though you may, and probably will, think I might better have left it alone, or followed it more faithfully."

Only two people besides Norton knew of the Sophocles' play: Mrs. Kemble, to whom FitzGerald sent a copy though at first he had thought he would not, and Aldis Wright, who, as FitzGerald explained in his letter to Mrs. Kemble, "would not have been of the party but that he happened to be here when I was too purblind to correct the few Proofs, and very kindly did so for me."[5] He explained to her about the choruses which he had not translated himself but taken from the translation by Robert Potter: "As I said of my own Aeschylus Choruses, I say of old Potter's now: better just take a hint from them of what they are about—or imagine it for yourself—and then imagine, or remember, some grand Organ piece—as of Bach's Preludes—which will be far better Interlude than Potter—or I—or even (as I dare think) than Sophocles' self!"[6]

FitzGerald called his play *The Downfall and Death of King Oedipus, A Drama in Two Parts, chiefly taken from the Oedipus Tyrannus and Colonaeus of Sophocles.* In his preliminary letter addressed to "My dear N——," FitzGerald apologized for the many changes he had made in the plays and explained his reasons in detail, declaring at the end, "While doing, as well as saying all this, I am sure you will understand that I am not pretending to improve on Sophocles, whether as a Poet or a Dramatist. As for Poetry, I pretend to very little more than representing the old Greek in sufficiently readable English verse: and whatever I have omitted, added, or altered, has been with a view to the English reader of To-day, without questioning what was fittest for an Athenian theatre more than two thousand years ago."

Judged on its own merits, FitzGerald's *The Downfall and Death of King Oedipus* is a gripping drama with two well-integrated parts. FitzGerald has tried his best to give a logical consistency to the action and to provide an acceptable basis for the incidents. For example, FitzGerald presents Oedipus throughout the play as a man in his prime rather than as an old man in the latter part. Sophocles, FitzGerald thought, had wished to heighten pathos by adding the weight of old age to blindness and calamity. But death by preternatural means would have greater dramatic force, in FitzGerald's opinion, if the catastrophe occurred in youth rather than at "a time of life when death in some way or another is inevitable."

FitzGerald has so infused the characters with life that his Oedipus approaches Lear in its tragic stature, and the eloquent words that FitzGerald puts into Oedipus's mouth are worthy of Shakespeare himself:

Oed.   O, not repenting or relenting, Thebes,
          But by an Oracle of Phoebus scared,
          Which told them that unless they get me home,
          To live what Life they leave me, and, when dead,
          Lie tomb'd outside—*outside*, I say—their Gates
          They shall not thrive in war against the foe,
          Whose walls shall overshadow what they lose.
          As Thebes shall find should ever strife arise
          Between herself and Athens, if their King
          Vouchsafe me that which I have ask't of him.
Thes.   But Thebes and Athens, friendly powers of old,
          What quarrel should arise to make them foes?

Oed.   O Son of Aegeus! to the Gods alone
Belongs immunity from Change and Death:
All else doth all controlling Time confound.
Earth waxes old: and all that from her womb
She brings to light upon her bosom dies,
And all is mutability between.
Ev'n so with Man, who never at one stay,
No less in mind than body changeable,
Likes what he liked not, loathes where once he loved,
And then perchance to liking turns again.
And as with man, with Nation none the less.
If now with Thebes and Athens all look fair,
Yet Time his furrow'd track of Night and Day
Pursues, wherein some grain of Discord dropt,
Perhaps no bigger than an idle word,
That shall infect his kindly Brotherhood,
And ripen'd Amity to rancour turn.
As one day—for I prophesy—shall be,
When my cold ashes underneath these walls
Shall drink the warm blood of my enemies—
Ev'n as they might upon this quarrel now,
Had Thebes not other foe to deal withal.

In his passionate outbursts, Oedipus rises to lyrical heights:

Oed.   You see not, for you know not how ere long—
How soon I know not, but not long, I know—
What others here now witness, standing round,
And some you see not watching underground,
Why from this spot, by which I first set foot,
I would not—no, not to be seated by
King Theseus' side in his Acropolis,
I would not move until I went to die.
Whether or not you guess my mystery,
Enough! You see I have unravell'd yours.
Begone! You lose but time and tongue—Begone!
And tell your people this on your return:
That, were the word from Delphi, and the word
From Thebes as false as you pretend it—yea,
False as yourself—I would not back with you;
No—not were all the Dragon brood of Thebes,
From the first armèd harvest of the teeth
That ancient Cadmus sow'd the field withal
Rais'd from the dust to join the living host

Who yell'd me forth—all these, and all the way
From Thebes to Athens grovelling at your heels
Back would I not with you—no, not to reign
Enthroned among them as I was before,
Much less a tainted leper like to lie
Outside your walls while living, and, when dead,
There huddled under as a thing accursed,
Save for the Victory that within me lies,
And shall but quicken as the body dies.
No; the same answer that I make to you,
Take home with you to all: on this same spot
Of earth, which now I stand a beggar on,
Beside this consecrated Grove, in which
By no delusive Inspiration drawn
I first set foot—I say, my Throne is here,
Deep-based as Hades, fix'd as Fate itself;
And this poor staff I long have lean'd upon
The Sceptre, wherewith from the world beneath
I shall direct the issues of the war
That shall determine wingéd Victory
To settle on the Land where tomb'd I lie.

In the following tranquil passages, one sometimes sees images reminiscent of the *Rubáiyát*. These beautiful lines are appropriately spoken by Antigone:

Ant.   And not far off I see the shining walls
And marble temple-fronts, and citadel,
As of some stately city: and the place
We stand on, as for some peculiar use
Sequester'd from the daily track of men,
Where a pure rill of water rambles through
Untrampled herbage, overshaded all
With laurel, and with olive, poplar-topt,
As you may guess from many a nightingale
About us warbling, well assured of home.

Oedipus himself can on occasion sound like a Persian poet:

Oed.   No more but this;
That, as I wander'd—not so long ago—
About the world begging my daily bread,
A little wind from Delphi wandering too

> Came up with me, and whisper'd in my ears
> That unless Thebes should have me back again,
> She would not thrive in arms against the foe
> That even then was knocking at her doors.

The play ends in a brilliant flash of light as the messenger describes
the death of Oedipus:

> The weeping Daughter turn'd away with us,
> Slowly, like those who leave a funeral pyre,
> With us our way re-tracing; until I,
> Seiz'd with a longing I could not control,
> Despite the word yet ringing in my ears,
> Look'd back—and saw King Theseus standing there,
> Stock-still, his hands before his eyes, like one
> Smit with a sudden blaze: but Oedipus
> There—anywhere—there was not—vanisht—gone—
> But, whether by some flash from Heav'n despatch'd,
> Or by His hand who through the shatter'd Earth
> Had summon'd him in thunder, drawn below,
> No living man but Theseus' self may know.

A choral epilogue to the play was added by FitzGerald in 1882. He
sent two versions of the chorus to Norton, telling him he could add
it to the second part or not as he pleased. "I cannot say much for it,"
he wrote on January 25 to Norton, "but it came together in my head
after last writing to you, while I was pacing up and down a Land-
ing-place in my house, to which I have been confined for the last ten
days by a Bronchial Cold." Except for this choral piece and two
other additions, the chorus is from Robert Potter's translation. C. E.
Norton had suggested that a good prose translation would be better
than Potter's chorus, and one can readily understand why. Turning
from FitzGerald's eloquent blank verse to Potter's unimpressive
chorus is sometimes like taking a false step and sliding down a hill.
Here, for example, is Oedipus musing over the secret of his birth,
and Potter's chorus:

Oed.   Forebode what ill it may,
        But I will solve the riddle of my birth.
        The Queen belike, of royal birth herself
        And haughty-minded as such women are,
        Resents her husband's baser parentage;

But I, regardless of the accident
That oft from royal blood provokes a slave,
I do account myself the royal heir
Of Destiny, who found me where I lay,
By man's blind foresight which defeats itself
Cradled to perish on Kithaeron's side,
And taking from a simple shepherd's hand,
So laid me in the lap of Royalty,
And through the days and years of human growth
Rear'd to the Kingly stature that I am.
And when, affrighted by vain prophecies,
From Corinth, and the throne prepared me there,
I fled, inalienable Destiny
Pursuing drove me but from throne to throne,
Till, doubling back my course to reach my height,
Now Thebes and Corinth claim me for their own.

Chorus

If a prophet's soul be mine
Aught illumed with skill divine,
By Olympus' sacred height,
Ere the morning's streaming light,
Thou, Kithaeron, shalt unfold
All this mystery round thee roll'd,
And with pride and triumph own
Oedipus thy foster'd son.
Then with joy would we advance,
Leading light the festive dance;
Teach thy woods with joy to ring,
And with transport hail our king.
Glorious with thy silver bow
Phoebus, these our joys allow!

FitzGerald's *Oedipus* will not please those who see no merit in
adaptation. To appreciate FitzGerald's translations, one must agree
with his point of view, and since his adaptations bear the stamp of
his characteristic style, one must also admire him as a poet and
writer. Regarded from a favorable point of view, FitzGerald's translations are literary variations on themes employed by playwrights
and poets before him. In his version of *Oedipus*, for instance,
FitzGerald emphasizes filial devotion in the figure of Antigone who
is alone with her father, FitzGerald having cut out Ismene's part

completely, and left all attention focussed upon Antigone. Regarded from an adverse point of view, FitzGerald's translations are distortions since they contain more of FitzGerald himself than the original. FitzGerald seems to have thought of his translations as original to the extent of the presentation and the style, both important in a literary work.

IV *Short Works*

FitzGerald's wide range of reading, which produced the translations, also inspired literary efforts on a smaller scale. One such composition is a poem in blank verse entitled, "The Two Generals." It consists of two parts; the first is a paraphrase from Livy of Lucius Aemilius Paullus' speech to the Roman people after his triumph over Perseus, king of Macedonia; the second is Sir Charles Napier's letter home following the battle of Meanee. FitzGerald had *The Two Generals* printed privately after his poem had been rejected by *Macmillan's Magazine* in 1868.

The first part starts with Paullus' lament over the death of his sons—

> With what success, Quirites, I have served
> The Commonwealth, and, in the very hour
> Of Glory, what a double Thunderbolt
> From Heav'n has struck upon my private roof,
> Rome needs not to be told, who lately saw
> So close together treading through her streets
> My Triumph and the Funeral of my Sons.

—and it ends with the mournful statement: "And Paullus is the last of all his Name."

Sir Charles Napier's letter, rendered into blank verse, contains some vivid descriptions:

> As I sate,
> My thoughts reverted to that setting Sun
> That was to rise on our victorious march;
> When from a hillock by my tent alone
> I look'd down over twenty thousand Men
> Husht in the field before me, like a Fire
> Prepared, and waiting but my breath to blaze.
> And now, methought, the Work is done,
> And well; for those who died, and those who live
> To celebrate our common Glory, well. . . .

The catalog in this poem of the variety of armed troops has a Victorian flavor:

> Imagine these in all varieties
> Of Uniform, Horse, Foot, Artillery,
> Ranged down the gaily decorated Tent,
> Each with an Indian servant at his back,
> Whose dusky feature, Oriental garb,
> And still, but supple, posture of respect
> Served as a foil of contrast to the lines
> Of animated English Officers.
> Over our heads our own victorious Colours
> Festoon'd with those wrencht from the Indian hung,
> While through the openings of the tent were seen
> Darkling the castle walls of Hyderabad;
> And, further yet, the monumental Towers
> Of the Kalloras and Talpoors; and yet
> Beyond, and last,—the Field of Meanee.
> Yes, there in Triumph as upon the tombs
> Of two extinguisht Dynasties we sate,
> Beside the field of blood we quench'd them in.

FitzGerald's two other short works met with better luck in regard to publication. An essay entitled, "Percival Stockdale and Baldock Black Horse" was accepted by the *Temple Bar* magazine for its January issue of 1880. A poem in couplets, "Virgil's Garden," which FitzGerald had written several years earlier, was also published by the same periodical in 1882. "Percival Stockdale" describes FitzGerald's journey in 1857 to Baldock in Hertfordshire to see the mill and tavern celebrated in a ballad popular in London in the eighteenth century. The ballad, written by a curate of Baldock, sings the praises of the daughter of the local miller and tavern owner. A hundred years to the day before FitzGerald's visit to Baldock, Percival Stockdale, a hack writer and would-be scholar, had journeyed to the town to see the beauty celebrated in the ballad. FitzGerald's essay, which gives an account of Percival Stockdale and his pilgrimage to Baldock, is a delightful example of FitzGerald's whimsical sense of humor. Percival Stockdale's memoirs apparently provided many amusing moments for FitzGerald, and in the essay FitzGerald shows the foibles of this very vain and very minor eighteenth-century personality who knew Samuel Johnson and David Garrick and who had had "the honour to write, and publish" in his *Miscellanies* the epitaph for Dr. Johnson's favorite cat, Hodge. FitzGerald describes Stockdale's friendship with the great man:

Johnson, humane and generous to all poor creatures, did all he could in behalf of poor "Stocky"—a kind of nickname which the owner thought Johnson only used to those he loved, though at the same time he (Johnson) seemed unaccountably "divided between a benevolence to my interest and a coldness to my fame." "He did not even mention *my* life of Waller in *his;* and thought my translation of Quintus Curtius 'rather encumbered with Latin idiom'; a fault that after the most impartial examination I own I could not find," and of which the public will one day decide whether such be the case or not.

FitzGerald was paid for the essay, an unusual occurrence for him. For his "Virgil's Garden," a short, pleasant poem, the magazine rewarded him with a dozen copies, which he thought was all he really deserved.

A more serious work that FitzGerald completed in 1879 was his *Readings in Crabbe.* For years FitzGerald had been preparing a selection from George Crabbe's *Tales of the Hall* (1819). He had known the poet's son well, and had written an obituary for him entitled, "The Reverend George Crabbe," which was printed in *The Gentleman's Magazine* of November, 1857. FitzGerald regarded Crabbe as a poet of great merit who had been unjustly neglected in both England and America. His favorite poem was Crabbe's *Tales of the Hall* which FitzGerald thought dealt with the follies rather than with the vices of man and with the comedy rather than with the tragedy of life. FitzGerald found a certain diffusion and carelessness in Crabbe's works, but he felt sure that a volume composed of Crabbe's best efforts would draw attention to his merit and restore him to his rightful place.

FitzGerald had tried to find a publisher in England or in America for such a selection but without success. In 1876, while reading Leslie Stephen's *Hours in a Library,* which included an evaluation of Crabbe, FitzGerald was roused to defend his favorite poet. "I think I could furnish L. S. with many Epigrams, of a very subtle sort, from Crabbe," he wrote to C. E. Norton on December 22, 1876, "and several paragraphs, if not pages, of comic humour as light as Molière. Both which L. S. seems to doubt in what he calls 'our excellent Crabbe,' who was not so 'excellent' (in the goody sense) as L. S. seems to intimate. . . . I wish some American Publisher would publish my Edition of Tales of the Hall, edited by means of Scissors and Paste, with a few words of plain Prose to bridge over whole tracts of bad Verse; not meaning to improve the original, but to seduce hasty Readers to study it."

Not finding any publisher for his volume, FitzGerald had the selections printed in 1879. The edition of three hundred and fifty copies was not put on sale until 1883. Leslie Stephen, who had received a copy of the *Readings in Crabbe*, pointed out to FitzGerald a passage in praise of Crabbe in Cardinal Newman's *Addresses to the Catholics of Dublin*. FitzGerald enlarged his preface, added the passage to it, and had two hundred copies printed in 1883. He died while the preface was being printed.

In his introduction to *Readings in Crabbe*, FitzGerald refutes the commonly held view that Crabbe lacked humor and was merely "a Pope in worsted stockings." To show Crabbe's skill for graceful expression and subtle humor, FitzGerald quotes lines like the following description of a middle-aged bachelor's realization of having fallen in love:

> Time after time the maid went out and in,
> Ere love was yet beginning to begin;
> The first awakening proof, the early doubt,
> Rose from observing she went in and out.

Undoubtedly, FitzGerald's familiarity with the locations of Crabbe's poems and his sense of identification with the personae had a great deal to do with his liking for the poet's work. In his article "Crabbe's 'Suffolk,' " which was published in *The East Anglian*, FitzGerald notes Crabbe's use of the Suffolk dialect, a subject in which FitzGerald himself was greatly interested. He quotes a passage from Crabbe to illustrate the use of the word "conceit" in the sense of conception, noun and verb:

> Still she came not home;
> The night grew dark and yet she was not come;
> The east wind roared, the sea return'd the sound,
> And the rain fell as if the world were drown'd.
> There were no lights without; and my good man,
> To kindness frighten'd, with a groan began
> To talk of Ruth, and pray; and then he took
> The Bible down, and read the Holy Book;

For he had learning; and when that was done,
We sat in silence—"Whither can we run?"
We said, and then ran frighten'd from the door,
For we could bear our own conceit no more.

This article on the dialect of Suffolk was among those that
FitzGerald contributed to *The East Anglian* describing the vocabulary of the seacoast. FitzGerald had always regarded the picturesque
language of the villages as purer than the English spoken in London
societies and as closer in strength to the English of Shakespeare and
Jonathan Swift. He had started collecting sea words and phrases
with the hope of publishing them someday. Two vocabularies of the
Suffolk dialect were in existence, *Suffolk Words and Phrases*, edited
by FitzGerald's old friend Major Moore, and *The Vocabulary of
East Anglia* by the Reverend Robert Forby, rector of Fincham,
Norfolk. Both of these vocabularies, however, were devoted mainly
to the language of the inland people and neglected to record the
dialect of the coastal regions. FitzGerald had thought of preparing a
composite of the two works and of adding to the volume the sea
phrases which he himself had collected. He abandoned the project
when a guide to Great Yarmouth and Lowestoft containing a vocabulary of sea words was published by J. G. Nall in 1866.
FitzGerald sent Nall his own list, asking him to use it in any future
editions of the book. Hearing no more of his sea words, he sent
them in 1868 to *The East Anglian Notes and Queries*. "On the
whole," he wrote to the editor, "I think if you print them as I send
them, it must be in some Christmas number, a season when even
antiquaries grow young, scholars unbend, and grave men are content to let others trifle." FitzGerald's "Sea Words" appeared in the
Christmas issue of *The East Anglian* for three years; he later had
them bound into pamphlets under the title of *Sea Words and
Phrases,* and distributed them among friends.

FitzGerald's gathered the material for his *Sea Words and Phrases*
mainly during the years of his friendship with Joseph "Posh"
Fletcher, a fisherman of Lowestoft, in whose noble bearing and
simple philosophy of life FitzGerald thought he saw true greatness.
Fletcher's physical resemblance to W. K. Browne, FitzGerald's
childhood friend and the prototype for *Euphranor's* ideal man, endeared him even more to FitzGerald, who referred to him as "a
Gentleman of Nature's grandest Type." To help his young friend,

FitzGerald went into partnership with him in 1867 by furnishing the money to build a lugger which Fletcher was to equip for herring fishing. The boat was called the "Meum and Tuum," but it was referred to by the sailors as "Mum and Tum." Although FitzGerald's venture into commercial fishing was undertaken for the benefit of his friend, their partnership placed too great a strain on their relationship. Moreover, FitzGerald's "noble savage" was given to over-indulgence in alcohol, a weakness that FitzGerald heartily despised; and his efforts to save "Posh" from himself only aroused his resentment. FitzGerald found excuses, however, for "Posh's" frequent lapses into drunkenness by remarking that the man, on the whole, was of royal nature.

FitzGerald's letters to his friends that extol "Posh's" greatness and nobility must have occasioned many a shake of the head over FitzGerald's sentimentality and his association with a man so much beneath him socially and intellectually. So great was FitzGerald's admiration for "Posh" that he commissioned Samuel Laurence, the painter, to prepare a likeness of Fletcher, one which he wished to hang on the wall beside the portraits of his two other best friends, Tennyson and Thackeray. The business partnership between FitzGerald and "Posh" was finally dissolved in 1870, but FitzGerald continued to help Fletcher financially. The only profit accruing to FitzGerald from the partnership seems to have been the vocabulary of sea words and phrases.

FitzGerald's vocabulary is not a dull listing of words and phrases; it is enlivened by interesting bits of reminiscence, poetry, and occasionally a wry dig at himself, as in this passage on herring luggers:

When first I knew Lowestoft, some forty years ago, the herring luggers (which then lay up on the beach, when not at sea), very many of them bore testimony to Wesley's visits to the place, and his influence on the people. . . . Beside the common family and familiar names, such as the William, Sarah Jane, Two Friends, Brothers, and such like; there were the Ebenezer, Barzillai, Salem, and many more Old Testament names; beside the Faith, Hope, Charity, &c., from later Revelation. A few vessels bore names in profane story—such as the Shannon (which, by-the-by, still *reigns*) after Sir Philip Broke's victory; there was even a William Tell (no longer reigning), whose effigies, drest in an English sailor's white ducks and blue jacket, pointed at the wind with a pistol from the mast-head. *That* was about the furthest reach of legendary or historical lore. But *now* the schoolmaster has been at sea, as well as abroad, and gone herring-driving—Bless me!

there's now a "Nil Desperandum," a "Dum Spiro Spero," and last, not least, a "Meum and Tuum"; though in the latter case it was very properly represented to the owners that the phrase being Latin, should properly run "Meum *et* Tuum. . . ."

Selections, such as the following, from FitzGerald's *Sea Words and Phrases* illustrate his ability to breathe life into any subject:

BARK. "The surf *bark* from the Nor'ard"; or, as was otherwise said to me, "the sea aint lost his woice from the Nor'ard yet," a sign, by the way, that the wind is to come from that quarter.

A poetical word, such as those whose business is with the sea are apt to use. Listening one night to the sea some way inland, a sailor said to me, "Yes sir, the sea roar for the loss of the wind"; which a landsman properly interpreted as only meaning that the sea made itself heard when the wind had subsided. . . .

SOU'WESTER. The very useful, but ugly, oilskin head-gear, used by fishermen, and making their comely faces really look very like some of the flat fish they deal in.

No glossary was needed to tell what a sou'wester is, nor, probably, for the little superstition attached to it. The sailor arriving from the north seas at nightfall, may go to his home, where the wife is sitting alone, thinking or not of him: just opening the door wide enough, he pitches his sou'wester into the room. The true good wife will run to the door at once, not minding the sou'wester. "But this may be old wives' mardle," said he who told me.

SPOOM. To scud before the wind.

Common in old writers: thus used by Dryden (who owes much of his vigour to his use of the *vulgar*):—
"When virtue *spooms* before a favouring gale,
My heaving wishes help to fill the sail."

This word we could well afford to keep in general use, though we scarce want its derivative.

V *Unfinished Works*

In one of the pieces contributed to *Notes and Queries* in 1861, FitzGerald had asked, "Why will no one reprint the whole, or a good abstract, of Dampier's fine *Voyages*?—and (now one is about it) all Dryden's Prefaces, which Johnson notices as things *sui generis* quite?" FitzGerald regarded Dryden as the finest prose writer of all, and he hoped that a publisher in England or America would agree to an edition of Dryden's prefaces. In 1877, FitzGerald wrote to his American friend, J. R. Lowell, suggesting that he might be able to get such an edition published in the United States, and perhaps in England too, as no English publisher would do this work "unless under some great name: perhaps under yours." FitzGerald completed a selection of his own, but he did not consider himself qualified to undertake the task of editor. He offered his collection to Aldis Wright to use as he wished in preparing an edition of the prefaces of "Glorious John." FitzGerald's selection, however, was never published.

FitzGerald left two unfinished works; one was a dictionary of the dramatis personae in the letters of Madame de Sévigné. He had started reading her letters in the summer of 1875, and had become thoroughly enchanted with the personality of the writer. To help keep track of the incidents, places, and people mentioned in her letters, he had prepared a large number of notes, but he did not put them in order. After his death, these notes and essays were edited by his grandniece Mary Eleanor FitzGerald Kerrich, and were published in 1914 under the title of the *Dictionary of Madame de Sévigné*.

The other work which FitzGerald might have contemplated undertaking was a biography of Charles Lamb. FitzGerald was always a great admirer of Charles Lamb, as was Thackeray. FitzGerald would often reminisce about how once young Thackeray, upon seeing a letter of Lamb's written to Bernard Barton, the Quaker poet, had reverently put the letter to his forehead with the exclamation, "Saint Charles!" Over the years, FitzGerald accumulated such a great deal of material pertaining to Lamb's life and works that he must have had in mind a biography of Lamb. But the only work relating to Lamb that he printed was a calendar of the important events in Lamb's life. He had prepared the calendar to help him keep track of the dates in Lamb's letters which had been published without regard to chronology. FitzGerald distributed his "Lamb Calendar" among his friends, one of whom, Frederick Pollock, called it, "Côtellete d'Agneau à la minute." In his later years, FitzGerald urged his friend Aldis Wright to utilize his material, the work of "Scissors and Paste," as he called it, to edit a life of Lamb. But he himself never carried out the project.

VI Bird-Parliament

The one translation which FitzGerald completed in his lifetime but left in manuscript form was the *Bird-Parliament,* a shortened version of a mystical allegory by the famous twelfth-century Persian poet, Farid uddin Attar. FitzGerald had started work on Attar's *Mantic uttair* before he became interested in the *Rubáiyát.* In his letter of January 22, 1857, written to Cowell in India, FitzGerald mentions borrowing a manuscript of Attar's *Mantiq uttair* from Napoleion Newton. With the help of Garcin de Tassy's analysis, *Memoire sur la poesie philosophique et religieuse chez les Persans,* FitzGerald had "nearly made out two thirds of it" in five weeks. FitzGerald found the *Mantic* not unlike *Salámán and Absál* in form, consisting of an allegory interspersed with short episodes. In his letter of January 23 to Cowell, FitzGerald included a translation in verse of one of the apologues. By March 12 of the same year, he had started putting his translation of the *Mantic* into shape, but he was not pleased with the result. "Anything like a literal Translation would be, I think, unreadable," he wrote to Cowell on that day; "and what I have done for amusement is not only so unliteral, but I doubt *unoriental,* in its form and expression, as would destroy the value of the Original without replacing it with anything worth reading of my own. It has amused me however to reduce the Mass into something of an Artistic Shape." In a March 20 addition to the same letter, FitzGerald noted: "To-day I have been writing twenty pages of a metrical Sketch of the Mantic. . . ." He then went on to express his view of Persian poets, one for which Oriental scholars have never forgiven him:

It is an amusement to me to take what liberties I like with these Persians, who (as I think) are not Poets enough to frighten one from such excursions, and who really do want a little Art to shape them. I don't speak of Jeláleddin whom I know so little of (enough to show me he is no great Artist, however), nor of Hafiz, whose *best* is untranslatable because he is the best Musician of Words. Old Johnson said the poets were the best Preservers of a Language: for People must go to the Original to relish them. I am sure that what Tennyson said to you is true: that Hafiz is the most Eastern—or, he should have said, most *Persian*—of the Persians. He is the best representative of their character, whether his Sáki and Wine be real or mystical. Their Religion and Philosophy is soon seen through, and always seems to me *cuckooed* over like a borrowed thing, which people, once having got, don't know how to parade enough. To be sure, their Roses and Nightingales are

repeated enough; but Hafiz and old Omar Khayyam ring like true Metal.
The Philosophy of the Latter is, alas!, one that never fails in the World.
"Today is ours, etc."

FitzGerald's view of Persian literature, expressed when he was
working on the *Mantic*, remained unchanged throughout his life;
the reason perhaps was that he gave up his Persian studies after his
Persian translations and thus his knowledge of the language remained at a rudimentary level. He was convinced that the Persians,
and perhaps Easterners in general, were backward and childlike and
that their literature naturally reflected a lack of sophistication that
bordered on the primitive. Compared to the Greek classics, which
FitzGerald had studied and hence appreciated greatly, the Persian
masterpieces were like cloying "sweetmeats" to him.

Generally clear-sighted in literary criticism, FitzGerald did not
realize that Persian literature appeared clumsy to him because his
knowledge of the language was inadequate. Secure in the belief of
his inherent English superiority, FitzGerald apparently could not
envisage the possibility that an Englishman could not master an
Eastern language, even though he had studied it for only a short
time. Although innumerable translators of the *Rubáiyát* after
FitzGerald have indicated his mistakes, they have usually failed to
realize that the superficiality of his knowledge of Persian and his
confidence in his superiority over the Persian poets enabled
FitzGerald to compose his masterpiece in his own way, unham-
pered by any bothersome doubts.

It must be said in FitzGerald's defense that he did not pretend to
be a scholar in Persian; he openly confessed that his translations
were only adaptations, done for his own amusement. What is sur-
prising is that he absorbed so much Persian in such a short time and
that he was able to detect merit as he did in his estimate of Hafez.
Most scholars would not agree with his coupling of Hafez with Omar
Khayyam—one, an acknowledged master; the other, a second class
poet in the estimate of many. In popularity, however, Hafez and
Omar Khayyam have proved to be among the most durable poets,
and they are almost equal in the affection of their readers.

By March 29, 1857, FitzGerald had "done" his "Will with . . . the
Mantic" and laid it aside. The same year, the French Orientalist
Garcin de Tassy published the Persian text of the *Mantic uttair* and
sent FitzGerald a copy. FitzGerald used this text to complete his
Bird-Parliament, which he mentions as having been done by

November, 1858. In 1862, a year before de Tassy published his prose translation of *Mantic uttair*, FitzGerald took up the poem again and put the finishing touches to it. He sent it to Cowell, asking that he submit it to the *Journal* of the Bengal Asiatic Society. Cowell, who was the Oriental Secretary of the Society, apparently did not think that the poem was suitable for the *Journal*, and he took no action in the matter. FitzGerald then asked Cowell to add elucidations and a short account of the poet to the *Bird-Parliament*, and have it printed at FitzGerald's expense. Cowell seems to have made no answer to these requests also, as appears from FitzGerald's letter to him dated August 5, 1863:

I don't hear from you: I rather think you are deterred by those *Birds* which I asked you to print (in my last Letter) with some Correction, etc., of your own: and which you have not found Time or Inclination to get done. But don't let anything of this sort prevent your writing to me now and then: no one can be more utterly indifferent than I am whether these Birds are printed or not: and I suppose I distinctly told you *not* to put yourself to any Trouble. Indeed I dare say I should only be bored with the Copies when they were printed: for I don't know a Soul here who would care for the Thing if it were ten times as well done as I have done it: nor do I care for Translation or Original myself. Oh dear, when I do look into Homer, Dante, and Virgil, Aeschylus, Shakespeare, etc., those Orientals look— silly! Don't resent my saying so. *Don't* they?

FitzGerald talked of printing the *Bird-Parliament*, but he never did so. It was only published after his death by his literary executor Aldis Wright.

Though the *Bird-Parliament* is similar to *Salámán and Absál* in that both deal with the mystical bond between man and God, in FitzGerald's version the imagery is reminiscent of his *Rubáiyát*. This similarity is understandable; for, at the time he was translating the *Bird-Parliament*, FitzGerald was also reading the *Rubáiyát*. One hears the echo of the *Rubáiyát*, for example, in these beautiful lines from one of the apologues:

> The Blaze that from my Harím window breaks
> With fright the Rabble of the Roadside takes;
> And ev'n of those that at my Portal din,
> Thousands may knock for one that enters in.

The *Bird-Parliament* describes, in the guise of an allegory, the quest of the soul for the Supreme Being. The story starts with the conference of all the birds of land and water, who gather to elect a leader and then set out on a pilgrimage to find their ruler, the mythical Seemurgh, which literally means thirty birds. The birds encounter great difficulties; the weak forego the journey; the strong persist, and perish on the way. Finally, only thirty birds are left. They reach the high throne; and, glancing up to see the Seemurgh, they discover their own reflection. FitzGerald ends his poem on this dramatic note; in the original, though the main story ends here, the episodes continue beyond this point.

Descriptions of the birds and the allusions to the myths surrounding them add color to the original poem; and the episodes, some of which are short philosophical reflections, break the monotony of the long allegory. FitzGerald's version is a fraction of the original in length; it does not include the opening invocations to God, to Mohammed, and to his successors, and it also omits the religious musings of the poet himself. Many of the episodes are omitted in the English version, as well as large sections of descriptive poetry. FitzGerald altered the story slightly in some places, and he dramatized it in others. He did not, however, distort the allegory: rather, FitzGerald's version gives what he himself called the poem, "A Bird's-Eye View of Faríd-uddin Attar's Bird-Parliament."

In places, FitzGerald's poem preserves a close fidelity to the Persian. The last two lines, for example, of the Owl's speech in praise of gold are a good rendering of the original: "He that a Miser lives and Miser dies,/At the Last Day what Figure shall he rise?" The episode that follows of the miser's appearing in the shape of a mouse is not only very close to the original but has also a dash of FitzGeraldian humor:

> A Fellow all his life lived hoarding Gold,
> And, dying, hoarded left it. And behold,
> One Night his Son saw peering through the House
> A Man with yet the semblance of a Mouse,
> Watching a crevice in the Wall—and cried—
> "My Father?"—"Yes," the *Mus*ulman replied,
> "Thy Father!"—"But why watching thus?"—"For fear
> Lest any smell my Treasure buried here."
> "But wherefore, Sir, so metamousified?"

"Because, my Son, such is the true outside
Of the inner Soul by which I lived and died."

FitzGerald's *Bird-Parliament* abounds in passages of lyrical beauty.
Sometimes one comes across lines of pure gold, as in this section on
the nightingale:

> Then came *The Nightingale*, from such a Draught
> Of Ecstasy, that from the Rose he quaff'd
> Reeling as drunk, and ever did distil
> In exquisite Divisions from his Bill
> To inflame the Hearts of Men—thus sang He—
> "To me alone, alone, is giv'n the Key
> Of Love; of whose whole Mystery possesst,
> When I reveal a little to the Rest,
> Forthwith Creation listening forsakes
> The Reins of Reason, and my Frenzy takes:
> Yea, whosoever once has quaff'd this wine
> He leaves unlisten'd David's Song for mine.
> In vain do Men for my Divisions strive,
> And die themselves making dead Lutes alive:
> I hang the Stars with Meshes for Men's Souls:
> The Garden underneath my Music rolls.
> The long, long Morns that mourn the Rose away
> I sit in silence, and on Anguish prey:
> But the first Air which the New Year shall breathe
> Up to my Boughs of Message from beneath
> That in her green Harím my Bride unveils,
> My throat bursts silence and *her* Advent hails,
> Who in her crimson Volume registers
> The Notes of Him whose Life is lost in hers.
> The Rose I love and worship now is here;
> If dying, yet reviving, Year by Year;
> But that you tell of, all my Life why waste,
> In vainly searching; or, if found, not taste?"

In one of the apologues is a theme which FitzGerald expanded
into the episode of the pots in the *Rubáiyát*. The dramatic dialogue
of the pots in the *Rubáiyát* was devised by FitzGerald from scattered quatrains. The apologue in Attar may have given him the idea;
he may have liked his version of the apologue and decided to make it
into an episode in the later *Rubáiyát*, or perhaps, in revising the

Bird-Parliament, he may have used the images of the *Rubáiyát.* In the apologue, the description of the potter at his wheel and of the clay being dug for him does not occur in that form in the original. FitzGerald also focusses attention on the vessel of clay and leaves out the main point of the Persian story, which is the exhortation to self-awakening. Jesus, who is the protagonist in the Persian version, is changed in FitzGerald's version to "the Prophet," presumably Mohammed:

> One day the Prophet on a River Bank,
> Dipping his Lips into the Channel, drank
> A Draught as sweet as Honey. Then there came
> One who an earthen Pitcher from the same
> Drew up and drank: and after some short stay
> Under the Shadow, rose and went his Way,
> Leaving his earthen Bowl. In which, anew
> Thirsting, the Prophet from the River drew,
> And drank from: but the Water that came up
> Sweet from the Stream, drank bitter from the Cup.
> At which the Prophet in a still Surprise
> For Answer turning up to Heav'n his Eyes,
> The Vessel's Earthen Lips with Answer ran—
> "The Clay that I am made of once was *Man,*
> Who dying, and resolved into the same
> Obliterated Earth from which he came
> Was for the Potter dug, and chased in turn
> Through long Vicissitude of Bowl and Urn:
> But howsoever moulded, still the Pain
> Of that first mortal Anguish would retain,
> And cast, and re-cast, for a Thousand years
> Would turn the sweetest Water into Tears."

The concluding section of *Bird-Parliament* describes the discovery of the Seemurgh by the thirty birds. FitzGerald's version is eloquent; and, except for portions, it is fairly close to the original. Dazzling light flashes through the poem; the drama heightens as the birds end their journey at the threshold of their sovereign. The imagery is from the original, though FitzGerald intensified the effect by curtailing the passage.

His explanation of the nature of the Deity and His relationship to man is, ironically, more involved than in the original. FitzGerald adds his own embroidery to the concept of oneness rather than follow the Persian, which uses simple and clear language to point out the inability of finite knowledge to fathom the infinite. In the original, the birds merge into infinity as the shadow dissolves into the sun. FitzGerald, who uses this metaphor elsewhere in the poem, offers a more elaborate description by mentioning, among other things, sin and remorse and retribution; and these somehow bring the *Rubáiyát* to mind. The following passage starts with the arrival of the birds at the mountain of Kaf where the Seemurgh is reputed to reside:

Till of the mighty Host that fledged the Dome
Of Heav'n and Floor of Earth on leaving Home,
A Handful reach'd and scrambled up the Knees
Of Káf whose Feet dip in the Seven Seas;
And of the few that up his Forest-sides
Of Light and Darkness where *The Presence* hides,
But *Thirty*—thirty desperate draggled Things,
Half-dead, with scarce a Feather on their Wings,
Stunn'd, blinded, deafen'd with the Crash and Craze
Of Rock and Sea collapsing in a Blaze
That struck the Sun to Cinder—fell upon
The Threshold of the Everlasting *One*,
With but enough of Life in each to cry,
On THAT which all absorb'd—
                    And suddenly
Forth flash'd a wingéd Harbinger of Flame
And Tongue of Fire, and "Who?" and "Whence they came?"
And "Why?" demanded. And the Tajidar
For all the Thirty answer'd him—"We are
Those Fractions of the Sum of Being, far
Dis-spent and foul disfigured, that once more
Strike for Admission at the Treasury Door."

To whom the Angel answer'd—"Know ye not
That He you seek recks little who or what
Of Quantity and Kind—himself the Fount
Of Being Universal needs no Count
Of all the Drops o'erflowing from his Urn,
In what Degree they issue or return?"

Then cried the Spokesman, "Be it even so:
Let us but see the Fount from which we flow,
And, seeing, lose ourselves therein!" And, Lo!

Before the Word was utter'd, or the Tongue
Of Fire replied, or Portal open flung,
They were *within*—they were before the *Throne*,
Before the Majesty that sat thereon,
But wrapt in so insufferable a Blaze
Of Glory as beat down their baffled Gaze,
Which, downward dropping, fell upon a Scroll
That, lightening-like, flash'd back on each the whole
Past half-forgotten Story of his Soul:
Like that which Yúsuf in his Glory gave
His Brethren as some Writing he would have
Interpreted; and at a Glance, behold
Their own Indenture for their Brother sold!
And so with these poor Thirty: who, abasht
In Memory all laid bare and Conscience lasht,
By full Confession and Self-loathing flung
The Rags of carnal Self that round them clung:
And, their old selves self-knowledged and self-loathed
And in the Soul's Integrity re-clothed,
Once more they ventured from the Dust to raise
Their Eyes—up to the Throne—into the Blaze,
And in the Centre of the Glory there
Beheld the Figure of—*Themselves*—as't were
Transfigured—looking to Themselves, beheld
The Figure on the Throne en-miracled,
Until their Eyes themselves and *That* between
Did hesitate which *Sëer* was, which *Seen:*
They That, That They: Another, yet the Same;
Dividual, yet One: from whom there came
A Voice of awful Answer, scarce discern'd
From *which* to Aspiration *whose* return'd
They scarcely knew; as when some Man apart
Answers aloud the Question in his Heart—
"The Sun of my Perfection is a Glass
Wherein from *Seeing* into *Being* pass
All who, reflecting as reflected see
Themselves in Me, and Me in them: not *Me*,
But all of Me that a contracted Eye
Is comprehensive of Infinity:
Nor yet *Themselves:* no Selves, but of the All
Fractions, from which they split and whither fall.
As water lifted from the Deep, again
Falls back in individual Drops of Rain
Then melts into the Universal Main.

> All you have been, and seen, and done, and thought,
> Not *You* but *I*, have seen and been and wrought:
> I was the Sin that from Myself rebell'd:
> I the Remorse that tow'rd Myself compell'd:
> I was the Tajidar who led the Track:
> I was the little Briar that pull'd you back:
> Sin and Contrition—Retribution owed,
> And cancell'd—Pilgrim, Pilgrimage, and Road,
> Was but Myself toward Myself: and Your
> Arrival but *Myself* at my own Door:
> Who in your Fraction of Myself behold
> Myself within the Mirror Myself hold
> To see Myself in, and each part of Me
> That sees himself, though drown'd, shall ever see.
> Come you lost Atoms to your Centre draw,
> And *be* the Eternal Mirror that you saw:
> Rays that have wander'd into Darkness wide
> Return, and back into your Sun subside."—

Though not an exact translation of the Persian, the passage just quoted, which is FitzGerald's conclusion to *Bird-Parliament*, offers a good summation of the mystical concept of oneness. The repetition of "Myself" emphasizes the theme of the passage; but it also has somewhat the effect of a chant. Artistically, the conclusion is a dramatic surge of action and imagery which subsides into the "Sun" of the last line. Why FitzGerald lost interest in the poem and did not have it printed as he did the others, is unclear. One can only conjecture that he may have been disheartened by Cowell's disapproval; but why he should have been deterred by criticism in this instance when he was not in regard to his other translations is difficult to say.

In 1867, when reading over Garcin de Tassy's prose translation of the *Mantic*, which he had not consulted when finishing his own version a year earlier, FitzGerald expressed his opinion about his version. In a letter to Cowell dated December 28 of that year, he wrote:

Here at Lowestoft, in this same row of houses, two doors off, I was writing out the Translation I made in the Winter of 1859. I have scarce looked at Original or Translation since. But I was struck by this; that eight years had made little or no alteration in my idea of the matter: it seemed to me that I really had brought in nearly all worth remembering, and had really condensed the whole into a much compacter Image than the original. This is what I think I can do, with such discursive things; such as all the Oriental things I have seen are. I remember you thought that I had lost the Apologues towards the close; but I believe I was right in excluding them, as the narrative grew dramatic and neared the Catastrophe. Also, it is much better to glance at the dangers of the Valley when the Birds are in it, than to let the Leader recount them before: which is not good policy, morally or dramatically. When I say all this, you need not suppose that I am vindicating the Translation as a Piece of Verse. I remember thinking it from the first rather disagreeable than not: though with some good parts.

Perhaps FitzGerald's view of the poem as "disagreeable" may have had something to do with his leaving it unprinted. Whether the poem itself left a disagreeable impression on him—though why this allegory should, when a similar mystical allegory *Salámán and Absál* remained his favorite—or whether the time at which he wrote the poem remained associated in his mind with disagreeable events, no one can say. The winter of 1859 could not have been a very happy time for him since the memory of his disastrous marriage would still have been fresh in his mind. *Salámán and Absál*, on the other hand, was always associated with the happy hours he spent with the Cowells. Whatever the reason, FitzGerald did not think highly of his *Bird-Parliament*, an opinion its readers find unjustified.

VII *FitzGerald's Letters*

Though the *Rubáiyát* remains the best known of FitzGerald's works, his letters must be regarded as his most delightful literary output. Written during the decades from early manhood to the day before his death, the letters have a spontaneity and a humor which surpass FitzGerald's more carefully indited literary compositions. Addressed to his friends, FitzGerald's letters were collected and published by his literary executor, William Aldis Wright, librarian of Trinity College. Wright seems to have been very cautious in his editing and selection, so much so that, when the letters were published, some of FitzGerald's friends complained that the collection did not do justice to him.[7]

In publishing FitzGerald's letters, Aldis Wright hoped to present FitzGerald as he had appeared to the small circle of his intimate acquaintances. He thought that the letters would explain more about FitzGerald than could any biography. He is right to the extent that FitzGerald's correspondence offers a wealth of information about his views on art, literature, and his famous contemporaries. Some of his literary opinions, which were regarded as eccentric by his friends, have been vindicated by time. One can see in his correspondence not only his overwhelming modesty and his great affection and loyalty towards friends, but also his clarity of vision, always tinged with humor, that could see the foibles not only of himself, but also of even the closest friends, and that could pronounce judgments based strictly on principle.

The early letters that start from the time FitzGerald left college after taking his degree in 1830, are mostly addressed to college friends, among them John Allen, later archdeacon of Salop; William Bodham Donne; and Bernard Barton, the Quaker poet. One finds in them the same felicity of expression and the whimsical, self-deprecatory humor that distinguish FitzGerald's later style. "I am sorry to say that I have a very young-lady-like partiality to writing to those that I love,"[8] he writes to Allen; ". . . I am an idle fellow, of a very ladylike turn of sentiment: and my friendships are more like loves, I think."[9] The letters are written in an easy, flowing, conversational style. "Here I live with tolerable ease," he writes to Allen from the country in a letter of April 28, 1839, "perhaps with as much as most people arrive at, and what if one were properly grateful one would perhaps call perfect happiness. Here is a glorious sunshiny day: all the morning I read about Nero in Tacitus lying at full length on a bench in the garden: a nightingale singing, and some red anemones eyeing the sun manfully not far off. A funny mixture all this: Nero, and the delicacy of Spring: all very human however." Over and over in his letters there are descriptions of the country and of the beauties of spring and summer flowers; and they sometimes read like the descriptions of the garden in the *Rubáiyát*.

Frequent references to Thackeray and Tennyson occur in the early letters. In 1839, Thackeray lived in the same street as John Allen, and FitzGerald would ask Allen to give his love to Thackeray "from your upper window across the street." These were the years when FitzGerald and Thackeray saw a great deal of each other, and one learns how they would amuse each other with descriptions of James Spedding's exceptionally high forehead:

That portrait of Spedding . . . which Laurence has given me: not swords, nor cannon, nor all the Bulls of Bashan butting at it, could, I feel sure, discompose that venerable forehead. No wonder that no hair can grow at such an altitude: no wonder his view of Bacon's virtue is so rarefied that the common consciences of men cannot endure it. Thackeray and I occasionally amuse ourselves with the idea of Spedding's forehead: we find it somehow or other in all things, just peering out of all things: you see it in a milestone, Thackeray says. He also draws the forehead rising with a sober light over Mont Blanc, and reflected in the lake of Geneva. We have great laughing over this.[10]

Twenty-three years later, after hearing of the death of Thackeray, whom he had not seen for years, FitzGerald wrote to Samuel Laurence, the painter: "Frederic Tennyson sent me a Photograph of W. M. T. old, white, massive, and melancholy, sitting in his Library."[11] A far cry from the laughing Thackeray of FitzGerald's youth.

The ability to present a picture in a few words is strikingly evident in FitzGerald's letters. Speaking of the fatal illness of his brother John's wife, he says, "While we are all living in this house cheerfully, she lives in separate rooms, can scarcely speak to us, or see us: and bears upon her cheek the marks of death. She has shewn great Christian dignity all through her sickness: was the only cheerful person when they supposed she could not live: and is now very composed and happy."[12]

FitzGerald's best descriptions, however, are of nature, which he appreciated with a painter's eye. He imbued bushes and birds with their own distinctive personalities. Remarking on the weather in February, 1844, he writes: "It blows a harrico, as Theodore Hook used to say, and will rain before I get to Woodbridge. Those poor mistaken lilac buds there out of the window! and an old Robin, ruffled up to his thickest, sitting mournfully under them, quite disheartened. For you must know the mild winter is just giving way to a remarkably severe spring." Thirty years later, he wrote to Fanny Kemble: "It has been what we call down here 'smurring' rather than raining, all day long, and I think that Flower and Herb already show their gratitude. My Blackbird (I think it is the same I have tried to keep alive during the Winter) seems also to have 'wetted his Whistle,' and what they call the 'Cuckoo's mate' with a rather harsh scissor note announces that his Partner may be on the way to these Latitudes. You will hear of him at Mr. W. Shakespeare's, it may be. There must be Violets, white and blue, somewhere about where he lies, I think."[13]

FitzGerald loved the country, and once when visiting London, wrote that he had "radishes to eat for breakfast of a morning: with them comes a savour of earth that brings all the delicious gardens of the world back into one's soul, and almost draws tears from one's eyes." In later years, he mourned the destruction of the green meadows and the pleasant walks in the name of progress and for the sake of profit. He complained to George Crabbe in 1861: "We are split up into the pettiest possible Squirarchy, who want to make the utmost of their little territory: cut down all the Trees, level all the old Violet Banks, and stop up all the Footways they can. The old pleasant way from Hasketon to Bredfield is now a Desert. I was walking it yesterday and had the pleasure of breaking down and through some Bushes and Hurdles put to block up a fallen Stile."[14]

He had a great love for the sea, and would go boating, taking his favorite books with him. ". . . I get to the Water," he wrote to Cowell, "where Friends are not buried nor Pathways stopt up: but all is, as the Poets say, as Creation's Dawn beheld. I am happiest going in my little Boat round the Coast to Aldbro', with some Bottled Porter and some Bread and Cheese, and some good rough Soul who works the Boat and chews his Tobacco in peace. An Aldbro' Sailor talking of my Boat said—she go like a Wiolin, she do! What a pretty Conceit, is it not? As the Bow slides over the Strings in a liquid Tune."[15]

In the 1870s Charles Eliot Norton and James Russell Lowell were added to the small number of FitzGerald's "epistolary friends." Once a month at the time of the full moon, he would also write to Fanny Kemble, who called these letters "lunacies." As one can see from his letters, age did not dim FitzGerald's powers of observation and expression, nor lessen his sense of humor. Speaking of Milton, he wrote to Norton in 1876: "I don't think I've read him these forty years; the whole Scheme of the Poem and certain Parts of it, looming as grand as anything in my Memory; but I never could read ten lines together without stumbling at some Pedantry that tipped me at once out of Paradise, or even Hell, into the Schoolroom, worse than either."[16] FitzGerald always remained a great admirer of Shakespeare, Scott, and, among contemporaries, Dickens. Describing a visit to Scott's Abbotsford, he declared, "I will worship him, in spite of Gurlyle,"—Thackeray's name for the historian—"who sent me an ugly Autotype of Knox whom I was to worship instead."[17] ". . . I never can forgive the Lakers all who first despised, and then patronized 'Walter Scott;' as they loftily called him: and He, dear, noble, Fellow, thought they were quite justified," he wrote to Norton in 1876: "Well, your Emerson has done him far more Justice than his own Countryman Carlyle, who won't allow him to be a Hero in any way, but sets up such a cantankerous narrow-minded Bigot as John Knox in his stead."[18] His correspondence with Norton, as with Lowell, was largely devoted to a discussion of books and writers, and to the relaying of news about mutual friends: "You have written to me, as I to you, more than has passed between myself and my fifty years old Friends for some years past," he once told Norton.[19] He would sometimes exchange books or articles with his American friends. Lowell was appointed United States ambassador to Spain in 1877, and several of FitzGerald's letters to him are addressed to his residence in Madrid. When the Spanish ambassador sent the Calderon Medal to FitzGerald, the latter felt sure that Lowell had suggested it.

FitzGerald became acquainted with Mme. de Sévigné's letters in the summer of 1875. Though he was at first repelled by her constant harping on "that eternal daughter of hers," he grew to like her immensely, and would quote her favorite remarks to his friends. " 'Ho! parlons d'autres choses, ma Fille,' as my dear Sévigné says," he wrote to Fanny Kemble in April, 1876. "She now occupies Montaigne's place in my rooms: well—worthily: she herself a Lover of Montaigne, and with a spice of his free thought and speech in her. I am sometimes vext I never made her acquaintance till last year: but perhaps it was as well to have such an acquaintance reserved for one's latter years. The fine Creature! much more alive to me than most Friends—I should like to see her 'Rochers' in Brittany."[20]

FitzGerald's last letter, which was written on June 12, 1883, was addressed to Samuel Laurence:

It is very kind of you to remember one who does so little to remind you of himself. Your drawing of Allen always seemed to me excellent, for which reason it was that I thought his Wife should have it, as being the Record of her husband in his younger days. So of the portrait of Tennyson which I gave his Wife. Not that I did not value them, as the most agreeable Portraits I knew of the two men; and, for that very reason, presented them to those whom they were naturally dearer to than even to myself. I have never liked any Portrait of Tennyson since he grew a Beard; Allen, I suppose, has kept out of that.

If I do not write, it is because I have absolutely nothing to tell you that you have not known for the last twenty years. Here I live still, reading, and being read to, part of my time; walking abroad three or four times a day, or night, in spite of wakening a Bronchitis, which has lodged like the house-hold "Brownie" within; pottering about my Garden (as I have just been doing) snipping off dead Roses like Miss Tox; and now and then a visit to the neighbouring Seaside, and a splash to Sea in one of the Boats. I never see a new Picture, nor hear a note of Music except when I drum out some old Tune in Winter on an Organ, which might almost be carried about the Streets with a handle to turn, and a Monkey on top of it. So I go on, living a life far too comfortable as compared with that of better and wiser men: but ever expecting a reverse in health such as my seventy-five years are subject to. . . .

Alluding to the wife of a friend, who was not expected to live beyond a year or two, he remarked: "Ah, Providence might have spared 'pauvre et triste Humanité' that Trial, together with a few others which (one would think) would have made no difference to its Supremacy. 'Voilà ma petite protestation respectueuse à la Provi-dence,' as Madame de Sévigné says. . . ."

The next day, Wednesday June 13, he set out to visit George Crabbe, at Merton where he was to meet Crabbe's sisters and "talk over old Bredfield Vicarage days." He spent the evening with the Crabbes, but he did not seem in his usual spirits. He went to bed early. The next morning, when he did not appear for breakfast, his host went to his room and found FitzGerald "as if sleeping peace-fully, but quite dead." FitzGerald had died in his sleep, as his mother and grandfather had done, and as he had hoped he would. He was buried in the churchyard at Boulge. The granite stone marker carried the epitaph that he had chosen for himself: "It is He that hath made us and not we ourselves."

In 1893, two rose bushes were planted at FitzGerald's grave. A bronze plate explained the significance of the roses: "This rose-tree, raised in Kew Gardens from seed brought by William Simpson, artist-traveller, from the grave of Omar Khayyám at Nishapur, was planted by a few admirers of Edward FitzGerald in the name of the Omar Khayyám Club, 7 October, 1893." In the ceremony that marked the planting of the roses, the members of the Omar Khayyam Club, which had been formed in London in 1892, read poems commemorating the Persian poet and his English translator.

William Simpson, who had brought the rosehips from Omar Khayyam's grave, had accompanied Sir Peter Lumsden and the Afghan Boundary Commission on their journey to Iran. In a letter to Bernard Quaritch, Simpson described his arrival at Nishapur on

October 8, 1884, and his visit to Omar's tomb: "For some days past, as we marched along, I have been making inquiries regarding Omar Khayyam and Nishapur; I wanted to know if the house he lived in still existed, or if any spot was yet associated with his name. It would seem that the only recognised memorial now remaining of him is his tomb." The Mongol invasion had reduced Nishapur, once the center of learning and a prosperous city, to a shattered little town. Simpson visited the tomb of Omar Khayyam, which he had imagined would be a grand edifice like the Taj Mahal but which he found was a humble grave without ornament. "Along the edge of the platform in front of Omar Khayyam's tomb I found some rose bushes," Simpson continues. "It was too late in the season for the roses, but a few hips were still remaining, and one or two of these I secured, as well as the leaves,—some of which are here enclosed for you; I hope you will be able to grow them in England,—they will have an interest, as in all probability they are the particular kind of roses Omar Khayyam was so fond of watching as he pondered and composed his verses." The rose bushes, planted at FitzGerald's grave, came from these rose hips of Nishapur. The roses had a double significance, for at the place of their origin is buried not only Omar Khayyam, but also Farid uddin Attar, whose mystical allegory, *Mantic uttair*, FitzGerald translated. Thus, at FitzGerald's grave, represented by the rose of Nishapur, are not only Khayyam the skeptic, but also Attar the Mystic.

If the greatness of a poet is judged by the quality and durability of his work, then by right, FitzGerald occupies a prominent place among the immortals of English literature. In his own lifetime, he gained no great fame, nor did he seek any. He set himself the task of introducing to his countrymen the works of foreign authors whom he admired, and he accomplished this task to his own satisfaction. He admitted taking liberties with his sources, but by allowing himself this latitude, he was able to re-create rather than translate, preserving the vigor and flavor of the original, as one sees in his masterpiece, the *Rubáiyát of Omar Khayyám*.

FitzGerald realized that the philosophy he incorporated into the *Rubáiyát* was not one that would be approved by the staid Victorian middle class. But the view that life is essentially a tragedy, ending as it does inevitably in death, was an ancient one, and was shared both by hedonists and mystics, with the difference that mystics found hope in a life beyond the earthly one. FitzGerald was by tempera-

ment an ascetic and inclined toward mysticism, as his interest in the
great Persian mystics Jami and Attar and his translation of their
poems shows. But FitzGerald was also a skeptic who could not
accept without question either religious or mystical beliefs about life
after death. In Omar's tragicomic approach, he found the expression
of man's dilemma and a philosophy not far removed from his own.
The hedonism of Omar, who was a mathematician and a
philosopher, was to FitzGerald a symbolic revolt against the sadness
of life, rather than a hedonist's celebration of the pleasures of life.
Omar's quatrains voice the universal struggle of man against fate.
FitzGerald recognized the timeless nature of Omar's ideas, and
expressed them in a form as appealing in English as Khayyam's
quatrains are in Persian.

FitzGerald's other translations have remained unrecognized;
perhaps the fact that they are called translations has obscured the
beauty of their diction and their dramatic force. The general expectation about translations is that, first, they are faithful replicas of the
original, and second, that they are usually not of high literary merit.
Readers do not look for artistic innovations in translations.
FitzGerald's translations are unlike others in both aspects. He diverges from the original, and he employs artistic devices sometimes
lacking in the original. The dramatic form of the *Rubáiyát*, for instance, its adherence to the unity of time, of place, and of character;
the three-tiered symbolism of time as one day, one year, and one
life; the double symbolism of place as the garden and the world, and
of the central character as the poet and all mankind; the evocative
use of color and light, and many of the rich metaphors are all
FitzGerald's own. Omar's ideas fit so naturally into FitzGerald's
framework that critics tend to overlook FitzGerald's contribution,
and some still judge his *Rubáiyát* solely on the basis of its fidelity to
the original.

FitzGerald accomplished the objective he was striving for: to en-
courage his readers to take up the study of the authors he had
translated. His translations from the Persian created interest in Persian literature, and brought Omar Khayyam greater fame in the
English speaking world than among his own countrymen.
FitzGerald's *Rubáiyát* was followed by translations both in verse
and prose by others, and FitzGerald's stanzaic form was employed
by other poets. None of FitzGerald's emulators and imitators,
however, achieved the perfect balance of language, music, and

philosophy which makes the *Rubáiyát* so easy to read and to re-member. In the twentieth century when the myriad demands upon man's attention leave him with little time for poetry, the exquisite brevity of FitzGerald's stanzas, their combination of deep truth and lyrical beauty, bode well for their continuing popularity. Like the ancient Persian ornaments of gold and gems, which were made small and precious so that their nomadic owners could carry their treasure wherever they went, FitzGerald's *Rubáiyát* will easily ac-company man as he travels through the centuries.

Notes and References

1. Francis Ann Kemble, *Records of a Girlhood* (New York, 1879), p. 83.
2. Francis Hindes Groome, *Two Suffolk Friends* (Edinburgh, 1895), p. 72.
3. William Aldis Wright, ed., *The Letters of Edward FitzGerald to Fanny Kemble* (New York, 1895), p. 9; dated February 27, 1872.
4. Gordon N. Ray, ed., *The Letters and Private Papers of William Makepeace Thackeray* (Cambridge, Mass., 1945), I, 165.
5. Ray, I, 167–68.
6. Ibid., I, 171.
7. Ibid., I, 388–89.
8. Ibid., I, 275.
9. Anne Ritchie, ed., *The Works of William Makepeace Thackeray, with Biographical Introductions by His Daughter* (New York, 1899), XVII, xliii.
11. William Aldis Wright, ed., *Letters of Edward FitzGerald* (London, 1894), I, 281.
12. Ibid., II, 50.
13. FitzGerald became a close friend of Frederick Tennyson as well, whom he came to know in the 1830s. After Frederick went to live in Italy, FitzGerald corresponded with him regularly. Frederick also was a poet; and FitzGerald who often urged him to publish a collection of his poems, declared that, except for Alfred's, Frederick's were the only poems by a living writer that he admired. Frederick Tennyson's poems were published in 1854. Frederick visited FitzGerald twice in Suffolk; though FitzGerald talked of going to see Frederick, who lived in a villa near Florence, he never did so. In his letters, FitzGerald spells Frederick without the final K.
14. Hallam Tennyson, *Alfred Lord Tennyson: A Memoir by His Son* (New York, 1897), I, 152–53
15. *Tennyson and His Friends*, p. 403.
16. F. R. Barton, ed., *Edward FitzGerald and Bernard Barton: Letters Written by FitzGerald 1839–1856* (New York, 1924), pp. 25–26.
17. Tennyson, *Memoir*, p. 155.
18. D. A. Wilson, *Carlyle on Cromwell and Others* (New York, 1925), p. 271.

160

19. *Letters of Charles Eliot Norton, with Biographical Comment by His Daughter Sara Norton and M. A. DeWolfe Howe* (Boston, 1913), I, 465.

20. *Edward FitzGerald and Bernard Barton*, p. 63; letter to Barton, March 17, 1842.

21. *Letters of Edward FitzGerald*, I, 33; dated May 23, 1835.

22. Ibid., 237; letter to Frederick Tennyson, May 4, 1848.

23. Ibid., 233; letter to Edward Byles Cowell, January 25, 1848.

24. William Aldis Wright, ed., *More Letters of Edward FitzGerald* (London, 1901), p. 22; letter to Cowell, November, 1848.

25. Hester Thackeray Fuller and Violet Hammersley, *Thackeray's Daughter: Some Recollections of Anne Thackeray Ritchie* (Dublin, 1951), p. 167. The letter by Emily Tennyson, dated July 16, 1889, was occasioned by Robert Browning's virulent attack on Edward FitzGerald in a poem published in the *Athenaeum* of July 13, 1889. In that year, William Aldis Wright had brought out a posthumous collection of FitzGerald's writings and letters. By an unfortunate oversight, he had not deleted a sentence from FitzGerald's letter to a friend in 1861, in which FitzGerald had remarked, "Mrs. Browning's death is rather a relief to me, I must say: no more Aurora Leighs, thank God!" That FitzGerald's remark was dashed off on the whim of the moment to a close friend is proved by his earlier statement in a letter to Cowell, in which he said that Elizabeth Browning's "Casa Guidi Windows" was a better poem than anything Tennyson had written in the 1850s. Browning, who happened to read FitzGerald remark about Elizabeth Browning's death, sent twelve lines of verse to the *Athenaeum* which ran as follows:

> I chanced upon a new book yesterday:
> I opened it, and where my finger lay
> 'Twixt page and uncut page those words I read,
> Some six or seven at most, and learned thereby
> That you, FitzGerald, whom by ear and eye
> She never knew, "thanked God my wife was dead."
>
> Ay, dead! and were yourself alive, good Fitz,
> How to return you thanks would pass my wits.
> Kicking you seems the common lot of curs—
> While more appropriate greeting lends you grace:
> Surely to spit there glorifies your face—
> Spitting from lips once sanctified by Hers.

This undignified attack on a dead man who could no longer defend himself brought forth protests from FitzGerald's friends. Among them was Emily Tennyson, who wrote the following letter to Anne Ritchie, who had herself written to Browning in defence of FitzGerald:

Thank you for your welcome letter. Yes indeed Edward FitzGerald's friends perfectly understand the spirit in which those unhappy words were written. He would have laid down his life to save hers, I think all unknown personally tho' she were to him. . . .
    I wish Aldis Wright had not only omitted those words, but I wish that he had told people that FitzGerald lived for a time in a house in his Father's park on five shillings a week that he might give the rest of what he had to the poor. A man so kind never would have written those words had he thought they would be made public, or misunderstood by him to whom they were addressed. (*Thackeray's Daughter*, pp. 167–68)

26. Hallam Tennyson, *Memoirs*, I, 253.
27. Ibid.
28. *Letters to Fanny Kemble*, p. 110; dated September 21, 1876.
29. *Edward FitzGerald and Bernard Barton*, p. 134; dated May 4, 1846.
30. *Letters of Charles Eliot Norton*, I, 439.
31. *Letters of Edward FitzGerald*, I, ix. Carlyle's regard for FitzGerald remained undiminished. Carlyle's niece, to whom in the last years of Carlyle's life FitzGerald would direct enquiries about Carlyle's health, wrote to FitzGerald after Carlyle's death that only a few days earlier she had told Carlyle of receiving a letter from FitzGerald, and Carlyle had said, "You must answer that." (FitzGerald's letter to Norton, February 20, 1881.)
32. Ibid., II, 344; dated May 12, 1883 to C. E. Norton.
33. Ibid., 105; dated February 21, 1842.

Chapter Two

1. *Letters of Edward FitzGerald*, I, 5–6.
2. George Cowell, *The Life and Letters of Edward Byles Cowell* (London, 1904), p. 41.
3. Cowell, pp. 59–60.
4. *Letters of Edward FitzGerald*, I, 232; letter dated January 25, 1848.
5. Cowell, p. 90.

Chapter Three

1. Wright, ed., *More Letters of Edward FitzGerald*, p. 33; letter dated April 4, 1853.
2. Pedro Calderon de la Barca, *El Pintor de su Deshonra, Nadie fie su Secreto, Luis Perez el Gallego, La tres Justicias en una, El Alcalde de Zalamea, Guardate de la Agua Mansa.*
3. Anon., "Six Dramas of Calderon. Freely Translated by E. FitzGerald," *Athenaeum*, September 10, 1853, p. 1063.
4. Richard Chenevix Trench, *Calderon: His Life and Genius, with Specimens of His Plays* (New York, 1856), p. 112.
5. Cowell, p. 101.
6. Anon., "Salámán and Absál: an Allegory. Translated from The Persian of Jámi," *Athenaeum*, August 2, 1856, pp. 957–58.

Chapter Four

1. Mary Eleanor FitzGerald Kerrich, "Memories of Edward FitzGerald," *East Anglian Magazine*, August, 1935, p. 84.

2. *Edward FitzGerald and Bernard Barton*, pp. 180–81.

3. Ibid., 182.

4. *Letters of Edward FitzGerald*, I, 328; dated April 22, 1857, to Mrs. Cowell.

5. Ibid., I, 336. Dated July 13, 1857.

6. Arthur J. Arberry, *The Romance of the Rubáiyát* (London, 1959), p. 81. Professor Arberry includes a number of FitzGerald's unpublished letters to Cowell, written while FitzGerald was translating the *Rubáiyát*.

7. Thomas Wright, *The Life of Edward FitzGerald* (New York, 1904), II, 202.

8. *Letters of Edward FitzGerald*, I, 345–46; dated September 3, 1858.

9. C. Quaritch Wrentmore, ed., *Letters from Edward FitzGerald to Bernard Quaritch: 1853–1883* (London, 1926), p. 6.

10. Alfred McKinley Terhune, *The Life of Edward FitzGerald* (New Haven, 1947), p. 210. This is the best documented biography of FitzGerald, and includes a number of unpublished letters.

11. *Letters of Charles Eliot Norton*, I, 426.

12. Ibid., I, 471.

13. Terhune, p. 212.

14. *Letters to Bernard Quaritch*, p. 32.

15. Ibid., p. 60; dated January 16, 1879.

16. FitzGerald was not the only poet to take liberties with his original. Matthew Arnold's "Sohrab and Rustum," which is widely regarded as recounting the episode of Sohrab from Firdusi's *Shah Nameh*, and is so described in anthologies of literature, differs widely in reality from the original version. Matthew Arnold put together the details of his story, not from any translations in English or in French of the *Shah Nameh*, but from short accounts of the episode of Sohrab in Sainte-Beuve's review and in Malcolm's *History of Persia*. For details of Arnold's debt to the latter, see my "Matthew Arnold's Version of the Episode of Sohrab," *Orientalia Suecana*, 16 (1967).

Chapter Five

1. *Letters of Edward FitzGerald*, II, 60–61; letter to Cowell, November 11, 1864.

2. *Letters to Bernard Quaritch*, pp. 36–37.

3. Ibid., p. 40.

4. Robert Potter, 1721–1804.

5. *Letters to Fanny Kemble*, p. 198; dated, February, 1881.

6. Ibid., pp. 201–02.

7. The letters were first published as part of *Letters and Literary Remains*, then separately.

8. *Letters of Edward FitzGerald*, I, 14; dated November [27, 1832].
9. Ibid., 30; September 9, [1834].
10. Ibid., 77–78; letter to Frederick Tennyson, January 16, 1841.
11. Ibid., II, 50; dated January 7, 1864.
12. Ibid., I, 35–36; letter to John Allen, July 4, 1835.
13. Ibid., II, 313.
14. Ibid., 19; dated May 20, 1861.
15. Ibid., 20–21; dated May 22, 1861.
16. Ibid., 193; dated February 7, 1876.
17. Ibid., 172; letter to W. F. Pollock, July 23, 1876.
18. Ibid., 194; dated February 7, 1876.
19. Ibid., 241; April 4, 1878.
20. *Letters to Fanny Kemble*, pp. 101–02.

Selected Bibliography

PRIMARY SOURCES

1. Works published during FitzGerald's lifetime

The Meadows in Spring. Athenaeum 193 (July, 1831), 442.

"Memoir of Bernard Barton." In *Selections from The Poems and Letters of Bernard Barton.* Edited by his daughter. London: Hall, Virtue and Co., 1849.

Euphranor, a dialogue on youth. London: William Pickering, 1851.

Polonius: a collection of wise saws and modern instances. London: William Pickering, 1852.

Six Dramas of Calderon. London: William Pickering, 1853.

Euphranor. Second Edition. London: John W. Parker and Son, 1855.

Salámán and Absál, an allegory. Translated from the Persian of Jámi. London: John W. Parker and Son, 1856.

Rubáiyát of Omar Khayyám. London: Bernard Quaritch, 1859.

The Mighty Magician. "Such Stuff as Dreams are Made of." Privately distributed. 1865.

Agamemnon. A Tragedy taken from Aeschylus. Privately distributed. 1869.

Rubáiyát of Omar Khayyám. Second Edition. London: Bernard Quaritch, 1868.

The Two Generals. Privately distributed. 1868.

Salámán and Absál. Second edition; privately distributed. 1871.

Rubáiyát of Omar Khayyám. Third edition. London: Bernard Quaritch, 1872.

Agamemnon. London: Bernard Quaritch, 1876.

Rubáiyát of Omar Khayyám and the *Salámán and Absál of Jámi.* London: Bernard Quaritch, 1879.

The Downfall and Death of King Oedipus. Privately distributed. Part I, 1880; Part II, 1881.

Readings in Crabbe. London: Bernard Quaritch, 1882. First printed and distributed privately in 1879.

Euphranor. Third Edition; privately distributed. 1882.

2. Collected and Posthumous Editions

Letters and Literary Remains of Edward FitzGerald. Edited by William Aldis Wright. 3 vols. London: Macmillan, 1889.

Letters of Edward FitzGerald. Edited by William Aldis Wright. 2 vols. London: Macmillan, 1894.

165

Letters of Edward FitzGerald to Fanny Kemble. Edited by William Aldis Wright. London: Macmillan, 1895.

More Letters of Edward FitzGerald. Edited by William Aldis Wright. London: Macmillan, 1901.

Letters and Literary Remains of Edward FitzGerald. Edited by William Aldis Wright. 7 vols. London: Macmillan, 1902–1903.

The Variorum and Definitive Edition of the Poetical and Prose Writings of Edward FitzGerald, including a Complete Bibliography and Interesting Personal and Literary Notes. Edited by George Bentham. 7 vols. New York: Doubleday, 1902.

Dictionary of Madame de Sévigné. Edited by Mary Eleanor FitzGerald Kerrich. 2 vols. London: Macmillan, 1914.

Edward FitzGerald and Bernard Barton: Letters Written by FitzGerald 1839–1856. Edited by F. R. Barton. New York: Putnam's, 1924.

Letters from Edward FitzGerald to Bernard Quaritch. Edited by C. Quaritch Wrentmore. London: Bernard Quaritch, 1926.

A FitzGerald Friendship: Being hitherto Unpublished Letters from Edward FitzGerald to William Bodham Donne. Edited by Neilson Campbell Hannay and Catharine Bodham Johnson. New York: William Rudge, 1932.

Rubáiyát of Omar Khayyám. Introduction by Thomas Yoseloff. New York: Fine Editions Press, 1957.

FitzGerald's Rubáiyát. Centennial Edition. Edited by Carl J. Weber. Waterville, Me.: Colby College Press, 1959.

SECONDARY SOURCES

ADAMS, MORLEY. *Omar's Interpreter.* London: Priory Press, 1911.

ARBERRY, ARTHUR J. *Omar Khayyám: a New Version Based Upon Recent Discoveries.* New Haven: Yale University Press, 1952. Translation in verse by Professor Arberry of the *Rubáiyát* of Omar Khayyam that were found in a manuscript dated 604 A.D. which was acquired by Cambridge University. Translation follows the metrical scheme used by Tennyson in *In Memoriam*, and keeps as close to the original as possible. The introduction is particularly informative. The Persian manuscript itself, however, is now considered to be a forgery.

————. *The Romance of the Rubáiyát: FitzGerald's First Edition Reprinted with Introduction and Notes.* London: Allen and Unwin, 1959. In his introduction, Professor Arberry includes a number of unpublished letters by FitzGerald which throw light on FitzGerald's method of translation.

ARNOT, ROBERT. *The Sufistic Quatrains of Omar Khayyam, in Definitive Form including the Translations of Edward FitzGerald, Edward Heron-Allen's Analysis, E. H. Whinfield, J. B. Nicolas.* New York: M. Walter Dunne, 1903. As the title states, the editor regards Omar as a

Sufi. The collection of translations, including an English version of Nicolas's French prose translation, and Heron-Allen's analysis, all in one volume, make this book a handy reference for the student.

BENSON, A. C. *Edward FitzGerald.* New York: Macmillan, 1905. A short biography; deals with FitzGerald's writings as well.

BROWNE, EDWARD G. *A Literary History of Persia.* 4 vols. London: T. Fisher Unwin, 1902. Standard work of reference on Persian literature; provides the student of FitzGerald's works with background material on the Persian poems FitzGerald translated.

COWELL, EDWARD B. "Omar Khayyam, the Astronomer Poet of Persia." *Calcutta Review,* March, 1858, pp. 149–62. FitzGerald quoted part of this article in his introduction to the *Rubáiyát.*

COWELL, GEORGE. *Life and Letters of Edward Byles Cowell.* London: Macmillan, 1904. Book includes a description of the friendship between FitzGerald and Cowell, who persuaded FitzGerald to study Persian.

DE POLNAY, PETER. *Into an Old Room.* London: Secker and Warburg, 1950. The biography contains interesting anecdotes about FitzGerald.

DE TASSY, GARCIN. "Note sur les rubâ'iyât de 'Omar Khaïyâm." *Journal Asiatique* (June, 1857), 548–54. De Tassy based his article on the transcript of the *Rubáiyát* that FitzGerald sent him.

DOLE, NATHAN HASKELL. *Rubáiyát of Omar Khayyám: English, French, German, Italian, and Danish Translations Comparatively arranged in Accordance with the Text of Edward FitzGerald's Version.* 2 vols. Boston: L. C. Page, 1898. The texts of the translations of the *Rubáiyát* in the languages listed in the title are given to provide comparison with the *Rubáiyát* of FitzGerald. The second volume consists of a series of appendices discussing the various aspects of the versions.

ELWELL-SUTTON, L. P. "The Omar Khayyam Puzzle." *Royal Central Asian Journal,* 55, Part 2 (June 1968).

———. "The Rubaiyat Revisited." *Delos,* 3 (1969).

FULLER, HESTER THACKERAY, and HAMMERSLEY, VIOLET. *Thackeray's Daughter.* Dublin, 1951. Includes description of Thackeray's friendship with FitzGerald.

GLYDE, JOHN. *The Life of Edward FitzGerald.* Chicago: Herbert Stone, 1900. Useful as an additional biographical source.

GRAVES, ROBERT, and ALI-SHAH, OMAR. *The Rubaiyat of Omar Khayaam: a New Translation with Critical Commentaries.* London: Cassell, 1967. Graves and his cotranslator claim that their version is based on a twelfth-century text owned by the family of Omar Ali-Shah. In a series of long-winded and pietistic elucidations, Graves attacks FitzGerald for subverting the true nature of the quatrains by Khayyam, who emerges in Graves version as a narrow-minded, humorless, and not very intelligent Sufi. The authoritarian pose affected by Graves and Omar Ali-

Shah has been very effectively unmasked in articles by a number of Oriental scholars, among them L. P. Elwell-Sutton of Edinburgh University, who points out their many errors, both interpretative and factual, and presents evidence to show that the eight hundred year old manuscript is a hoax.

GROOME, FRANCIS HINDES. *Two Suffolk Friends*. Edinburgh: Blackwood, 1895. Recollections of Groome's father's friendship with FitzGerald.

HERON-ALLEN, EDWARD. *The Ruba'iyat of Omar Khayyám: A Facsimilie of the Manuscript in the Bodleian Library at Oxford, with a Transcript into Modern Persian Characters*. London: H. S. Nichols, 1898. Heron-Allen provides a literal prose translation of the *Rubáiyát* to allow the reader to gauge the degree of FitzGerald's fidelity to his source. Heron-Allen was the first to make a detailed search for the quatrains that FitzGerald actually used in his version. In this book, Heron-Allen lists the variant readings for each stanza in the Bodleian manuscript, using for comparison a number of extant copies of the *Rubáiyát*. His notes are placed side by side with the reproductions of the Bodleian quatrains; he also provides a transcript of the stanzas in a clearer hand, followed on the same page by his own prose translation.

INCE, RICHARD B. *Calverley and Some Cambridge Wits of the Nineteenth Century*. London: Richard and Toulmin, 1929. Contains a well-written chapter on FitzGerald.

KEMBLE, FRANCES ANN. *Records of a Girlhood*. New York: Holt, 1879.

———. *Records of Later Life*. New York: Holt, 1883.

———. *Further Records*. New York: Holt, 1891. Mrs. Kemble's biography offers a picture of her times; includes reminiscences of the FitzGerald family.

KERRICH, MARY ELEANOR FITZGERALD. "Homes and Haunts of Edward FitzGerald." *Blackwood's Magazine* 174 (1903), 452–93.

———. "Edward FitzGerald, a Personal Reminiscence." *Nineteenth Century* 65 (1909), 461–69. Mary Kerrich is FitzGerald's grandniece.

LOUNSBURY, THOMAS R. *The Life and Times of Tennyson*. New York: Russell and Russell, 1962. Includes material on FitzGerald's friendship with Tennyson.

NICOLAS, J. B. *Les Quatrains de Khèyam*. Paris: 1867. Nicolas supported the view that Omar was a Sufi; FitzGerald disagreed with him in the preface to the second edition of the *Rubáiyát*.

NORTON, CHARLES ELIOT. "Nicolas's Quatrains de Khèyam." *North American Review*, October, 1869, pp. 565–84. First review of FitzGerald's *Rubáiyát*, that brought it to the attention of the public, especially in the United States.

NORTON, SARA, and HOWE, M. A. DEWOLFE. *Letters of Charles Eliot Norton*. 2 vols. Boston: Houghton Mifflin, 1913. Includes, among other references to FitzGerald, Carlyle's views on him.

POTTER, AMBROSE GEORGE. *A Bibliography of the Rubáiyát of Omar Khayyám.* London: Ingpen and Grant, 1929.

RAY, GORDON N. *The Letters and Private Papers of William Makepeace Thackeray.* 4 vols. Cambridge, Mass.: Harvard University Press, 1945. The letters show the close friendship between Thackeray and FitzGerald in the 1830s and 1840s.

————. *Thackeray.* 2 vols. New York: McGraw-Hill, 1955–1958. Includes material on the friendship between Thackeray and FitzGerald.

RITCHIE, ANN., ed. *The Works of William Makepeace Thackeray: with Biographical Introductions by His Daughter.* 25 vols. New York: Harper's, 1899. The introduction to Volume 17 is devoted to FitzGerald's friendship with Thackeray.

RITCHIE, HESTER THACKERAY. *Thackeray and His Daughter.* New York: Harper's, 1924. Includes material on Thackeray's friendship with FitzGerald.

TENNYSON, CHARLES. *Alfred Tennyson.* New York, 1949. Tennyson's biography by his grandson; describes the friendship between Tennyson and FitzGerald.

TENNYSON, HALLAM. *Alfred Lord Tennyson.* 2 vols. New York: Macmillan, 1897. Includes description of Tennyson's friendship with FitzGerald.

————, ed. *Tennyson and His Friends.* London: Macmillan, 1911. A collection of essays; includes material on the friendship between Tennyson and FitzGerald.

TERHUNE, ALFRED MCKINLEY. The Life of Edward FitzGerald. New Haven: Yale University Press, 1947. Best biography of FitzGerald published so far. A comprehensive collection of FitzGerald's letters and papers edited by Professor Terhune is due to be published.

THOMPSON, EBEN FRANCIS. *Edward FitzGerald's Rubáiyát of Omar Khayyám, with a Persian Text, a Transliteration, and a close Prose and Verse Translation.* Privately printed, 1907. The volume contains the Persian quatrains believed to be FitzGerald's sources, FitzGerald's version, and Thompson's translations in prose and verse, which illustrate why FitzGerald preferred literary quality to fidelity.

TRENCH, RICHARD CHENEVIX. *Calderon: His Life and Genius.* New York: Redfield, 1856. In the introduction to this book, Trench praised FitzGerald's translation of Calderon's plays.

TUTIN, J. R. *A Concordance to FitzGerald's Translation of the Rubáiyát of Omar Khayyám.* London: Macmillan, 1900. Useful reference for the student.

WALKER, HUGH. *The Literature of the Victorian Era.* Combridge: Cambridge University Press, 1910. For students who want information on FitzGerald's era.

WHINFIELD, E. H. *The Quatrains of Omar Khayyam: the Persian Text with an English Verse Translation.* London: Trübner, 1883. Whinfield offers

a selection of Omar Khayyam's quatrains which he has chosen from a
number of extant manuscripts; he gives his verse translation of each
quatrain on the opposite page.

WILSON, D. A. *The Life of Thomas Carlyle.* 6 vols. New York: Dutton,
1923–1934. Includes material on FitzGerald's friendship with Carlyle.
WRIGHT, THOMAS. *The Life of Edward FitzGerald.* 2 vols. New York:
Scribner's, 1904. Interesting and detailed biography, but has some
factual inaccuracies.

Index